# Preface

I thought I would find you here. Curious? You should be. Negotiation is fundamental to your life and the way you distribute, create, protect, resolve, and manage anything of value. It is central to the viability of every business, for even non-profit-making organizations. It has delivered peace in war, resolved bedtime tantrums with our children, helped avoid millions of court cases, and has probably helped save a few marriages along the way too. It is how you resolve differences and form agreements based on mutually acceptable terms. It can represent the difference between viability and insolvency, profit making or loss, growth or decline; such is the power of the outcomes.

Great negotiators often go unnoticed. They are not interested in winning or glory. They have an attitude of mind which is focused on the hard work of building agreements and protecting this work through the necessary confidentiality which follows. However, great negotiators – and perhaps you – recognize that the return on time invested is dramatic, perhaps in relationships, time saved, risk reduced, profit made or even dilemmas resolved. No other skill offers so much value in return for competent performance.

In this book I have set out to provide you with an insight into negotiation from a practitioner's perspective. The art and science of negotiation is an interactivity that is influenced by culture, ever-changing circumstances, expectation, capability, and personal chemistry. The Complete Skilled Negotiator is an individual who has both the skills and mindset to do that which is appropriate to their circumstances and the ability to maximize opportunity during each and every negotiation. It can be the most rewarding of skills to exercise and the most nerve-racking. Is it any wonder that to provide a standard which helps everyone to negotiate more effectively has proved such a challenge to so many in the past? Yet simple disciplines, proactive planning, and a clear, conscious state of mind can provide a significant uplift in what you can achieve.

So what do I mean by a standard? *The Negotiation Book* covers the traits and behaviors associated with the Complete Skilled Negotiator. I use the word complete rather than successful because who are we to judge if your performances are as successful as they might be? We will never know. The standard also refers to a clock face model which provides a way of differentiating the range of ways we negotiate in a dynamic, capitalist market. Importantly it also recognizes that although the concept of power, process, and behavior have much to do with performance, so does the psychology, self-discipline, and human interaction which make up the framework. The standard is not here to restrict but to empower you as a Complete Skilled Negotiator to negotiate that which is possible… given those opportunities you are presented with.

The experience I have gained from practical hands-on involvement in having negotiated with some of the largest corporations on the planet including P&G, Walmart, Morgan Stanley, Unilever, GE, and Vodafone has helped me to provide this account of the standard which has been adopted in the business world. I have also been privileged to work with dozens of highly skilled negotiation practitioners at The Gap Partnership who have negotiated with, advised, and developed hundreds of such organizations globally. It is this experience which has helped us to crystallize what our clients have come to call "The Standard" for negotiating.

# CHAPTER 1

# So You Think You Can Negotiate?

## INTRODUCTION

Negotiation affects every part of our lives: the things we buy, the services we use, the holidays we book and the bread that we eat all come at a price. The price that the consumer pays for products and services is usually the outcome of what has been negotiated between two or more parties. So the next time the price of chocolate cookies increases by 10 cents you may want to think: is that inflation, a material cost price increase, a price repositioning against another chocolate cookie manufacturer, or has there been a negotiation between the supplier and the retailer resulting in a price increase? If there has, it may have involved a broad range of issues such as the funding of a special promotion, a change in the agreed payment terms, perhaps a pack size change or even something as simple as the packaging being made from a different material.

In *The Negotiation Book* I have set out to provide a philosophy on negotiation, which is not prescriptive, but aims to provide the necessary insights for you to get better deals by being aware that it is you who are responsible for making decisions based on your own judgement. The amount of time people actually spend negotiating is very small in the context of their whole job and yet the consequences of their performance during negotiations will often distinguish how successful they are. In this book, I have set out to provide you with both the questions and, of course, the answers that will promote your appetite and motivate you to become a great negotiator. This book is about *you* gaining more value from every agreement you're involved in, understanding what to do, when to do it and, most importantly, providing you with the inspiration to do it.

## SO WHAT IS NEGOTIATION?

Negotiation is a word, a process and an art. It evokes complex feelings for anyone faced with the prospect of having to negotiate an agreement. However, it is fundamental to how business gets done and takes place millions of times a day around the world. If you can take control of yourself, your values and prejudices, your need for fairness and your ego, you may start to realize the best possible outcomes in your negotiations. The biggest challenge here is not in educating you in how to be a better negotiator but motivating you to change the way you think about negotiations and yourself. Of the many thousands of negotiation workshops I have provided at The Gap Partnership, the greatest change I see clients make, as they develop their ability to negotiate, is that of self-awareness. Learning about negotiation is an exercise in self-awareness because understanding yourself and what effect a negotiation can have on you, enables you to accommodate the pressures, dilemmas and stresses that go with it. Self-awareness helps us to recognize why we do the things we do and the effect this has on our results. This in itself can be very motivating. It also helps us adapt our approach and our behavior to suit each negotiation rather than trying to make one approach fit every situation, simply because it suits our personal style.

### *Why get motivated?*

So many aspects of our lives are influenced by agreements with others, both personally and professionally. Invariably, our ability to negotiate the best outcomes will directly influence our success in life, however you measure success.

Success in negotiation can be measured in so many ways. For example, in relative terms.

- Did I get a better deal than last time?
- Did I get a better deal compared with what was on offer elsewhere, in terms of cost and inconvenience?
- Did I prevent the negotiation from deadlocking, which could have meant being faced with lots of undesirable issues to sort out?

Other measurements of success include the financial value, risk reduction, or even how far you managed to move the other party from their opening position. Depending on how you are measured or what objectives you are trying to achieve there may well be other **success criteria**. Whatever they are, you will need to be motivated to perform and that means using a wide range of skills in your negotiations.

**success criteria**
These will vary from negotiation to negotiation. They can be singular, such as securing the right price; or more comprehensive, such as "total value," however this may be calculated.

### *Why bother negotiating?*

Just because everything is negotiable doesn't mean that everything has to be negotiated. The value of your time versus the potential benefit that can be achieved by negotiating is always a consideration. Why spend ten minutes negotiating over the price of a $10 notebook when you normally make $100 an hour? So you may save $2, that's 20 cents a minute! However, if it is your next car and a 5% saving could equate to $1500, the time is probably worth investing.

An understanding with your wife or husband, or work colleague, has to have some give and take without which you might be regarded as inflexible or just plain difficult to deal with; so everything may be negotiable but that doesn't mean that you have to negotiate everything. However, there will be situations involving more important decisions where you are mutually dependent and yet hold different views. When an agreement needs working through, ultimately effective negotiation will help provide not only a solution but potentially a solution that both of you are motivated to carry through.

**volume threshold**

This can relate to a minimum order required for other benefits to be realized. The order may need to exceed a volume threshold of 1000 before discount levels become applicable.

There is no other skill set that can have such an immediate and measurable level of impact on your bottom line than negotiation. A small adjustment to the payment terms, the specification, the **volume threshold**, or even the delivery date, will all impact on the value or profitability of the agreement. Understanding the effects of these moves, and the values they represent to you from the outset, is a critical part of planning (see Chapter 9). The skill in building enhanced agreements through trading off against different interests is called negotiation. In the business context it is known as the skill of profit maximization.

So, effective negotiation provides the opportunity to build or dissolve value – but what does value *really* mean? It can be too easy just to focus on the price. The question of "how much?" is one, transparent, measurable issue and because of this, is also the most contentious issue in the majority of negotiations.

Yet price is but *one* **variable** you can negotiate over. It *is* possible to get a great price and feel as though you have won and yet get a very poor deal at the same time. For example, because the item did not arrive on time, or it fell apart after being used twice, or it had no flexibility about it and so on. (Ever heard the saying "you get what you pay for"?)

**variable**
This can be a price, an issue, or an agenda item and refers to something which needs to be agreed.

In negotiation, your ego and your competitiveness will fuel this need to "win," especially where there is a sense of competition involved. However, negotiating agreements is not primarily about competing or winning; it is about securing the best value. This means understanding:

- what the other person or party thinks;
- what they do; and
- how that affects possibilities.

As a Complete Skilled Negotiator your focus needs to be on what is important to the other party: their interests, their priorities, their options, deadlines and **pressure points**. Try to see the deal as they see it. If you set out to understand them and their motivations, you may be able to use these insights to your advantage and, ultimately, increase the value of the deal for

**pressure points**
Pressure points are things or circumstances which influence the other party's thinking or behavior.

yourself. Being driven to beat the other party will distract you from your main objective, which is usually to maximize opportunity.

### *Becoming proactive*

As a consciously competent negotiator your first task is to be proactive. That is, take control of the way you negotiate and map out the issues to negotiate each agreement in a way that will serve your objectives. Try to be honest with yourself when deciding or agreeing on what these are. Remember, price is only one element of the deal and winning on price may not result in your attracting the best deal. You may need cooperation to the point where the other party not only agrees to go ahead but is also prepared to *honor* their commitment, in which case you will also need to plan and prepare a range of variables and an appropriate process, and get inside their head. Becoming proactive is about getting inside their head and not about winning. There is absolutely no place for your ego in your negotiations. The single thing that matters is the **total value**, or the real value, however you may define this.

**total value**

This is where true value lies and where you, the negotiator, should focus. In fact, it is often as well to let the other person "win" on price, whilst you focus on the *overall* value. The value you can create this way can far exceed "winning" on price – even when you are working with fixed budgets.

### *Becoming comfortable with being uncomfortable*

The person on the other side of the negotiating table may well take up a tough position, which could make you feel challenged or competitive. Becoming *more* comfortable in situations like this, where you are also likely to experience feelings of pressure, tension and anxiety, must be one of the most important prerequisites of a skilled negotiator. Without this, our thinking and performance can

**CASE STUDY**

The new manager of a local German hockey team wanted to take personal responsibility for purchasing their team's new home kit in preparation for the new season. The manager took the time to meet with the team's sponsors to agree the design and then arranged to meet with the kit suppliers who the team had sourced from historically to place an order. During the meeting with the kit suppliers the new manager negotiated hard over the price he was prepared to pay. He demanded and secured a 15% discount on the prices paid as compared to the last batch ordered 12 months before. They became so tied up in the haggling process, other issues such as specification (color, font and stitching of names on the shirts), delivery dates and the exact mix of sizes required were all overlooked. These details were all provided at a later date by email when the order was confirmed, yet all of these issues turned out to be critical. The shirts finally arrived two weeks into the new season and were short of four small sizes required. By the time these issues had been dealt with, a quarter of the season had passed, the sponsors refused their sponsorship obligations and the manager's credibility was badly affected. All for what turned out to be a €500 saving!

become compromised. So a negotiator needs to recognize that, by negotiating, we are involved in a process and the people you negotiate with need time to adjust as part of engaging on this process. Typically this is when:

- any new risks, obligations, conditions, or consequences are presented; and
- any new proposals that you make which materially change the value of the agreement.

In business meetings people can become frustrated, emotional and upset if they feel that you are simply being irrational or unfair with your proposals. Some will even walk away before considering the consequences.

For this reason, the more experienced the negotiator you are working with, the less chance you will have of a deadlocked conversation. They are more likely to understand that they are involved in a process and that nothing is agreed until everything is agreed. In fact, their confidence means that you are more likely to get a better deal than when you attempt to negotiate with an untrained negotiator. Many of my clients insist that their suppliers attend the same training in negotiation as they do as part of ensuring that both parties work towards maximizing total value rather than becoming distracted by short-term gains and/or trying to win.

## THE NEED FOR SATISFACTION

Everyone likes to secure a bargain; to buy something at a better price than was available before. You only have to visit department stores on 27 December to witness the effect that securing a bargain can have on people's behavior. Such can be the frenzy that it is not unknown for violence to be used where one person feels another has pushed ahead of them in the queue. Many people just can't help themselves when there's a good bargain to be had. In extreme cases people will buy things they don't want or even need if the price is right.

### *What is the right price?*

The popular TV programme *The Price is Right* that ran through the 1990s pitched people against each other to name the retail price of everyday items ranging from TVs and freezers to holidays. The challenge was simply to guess the retail price of the item presented to you more accurately than the other competitors. Even on these common items which are continuously advertised, more often the price guessed was wrong and often by more than 25%.

In business, what is the right price? The answer depends on a whole range of other issues which, of course, need to be negotiated. So how do you manage the other party's need for satisfaction? That is, their natural need to feel as though they got a better deal than was originally available.

- Do you start out with an extreme opening on price?
- Do you introduce conditions that you are ready to concede on?
- Do you build in red herrings (issues which are not real, that you can easily, and expect to, concede)?

The psychological challenge here is providing the other party with the satisfaction of having achieved, through hard work, a great deal for *themselves*. In other words letting them win, or, letting them have *your* way.

### *Inside the other person's head*

Effective negotiators are motivated by curiosity and have a desire to understand "the way it is," from inside the other party's head. Without insight, you will remain in a state that we at The Gap Partnership call "being inside your own head," and that is a dangerous place to be during negotiation. If you really want to negotiate effectively, you first have to get your thinking this way round. Honesty with yourself, the situations you face, and a commitment to do what is appropriate, will require you to work on the emotional challenges you will face. It will be your own commercial pressures (those things which you are measured against or are accountable for) that will require you to operate as a "conscious competent negotiator" if you are to take control (see Challenge 1, later in this chapter).

## NEGOTIATING VERSUS SELLING

It is a commonly held view that a good "sale" will close itself and that negotiation follows when outstanding differences remain. However, negotiation as a skill and as a process is fundamentally different from selling. Whether you sell ideas, services or products, selling is selling, and it has no place in negotiation. To sell is to promote the positives, the reasons, to align the need to the solution. It requires explanation, justification and a rational case. "The gift of the gab" is associated with the salesman who has an answer for everything. Negotiation does not.

**silence**

Silence can also serve to strengthen your position during negotiation: the other person may seek to fill that silence with offers, or information, or in some cases simply capitulate as the silence becomes too much to bear.

Although relationships can be important, as is a climate for cooperation (without which you have no discussion), the behavior of the Complete Skilled Negotiator also involves **silence**, where appropriate. That means listening to everything the other party is saying, understanding everything they are not saying and working out their true position.

Negotiation involves planning, questioning, listening, and making proposals, but it also requires you to recognize when the selling has effectively concluded and the negotiation has begun. Once you start negotiating you have to stop selling. If you find yourself selling the benefits of your proposals during a negotiation, you are demonstrating a weakness. Selling once the negotiation has begun suggests that you don't feel that your proposals are strong enough and that they require further promoting which is what you are in the process of doing. Without realizing it you are actually telling them that you are feeling weak. The more you talk, the more you are likely to make a concession.

So, recognizing when the change from selling to negotiating has taken place is critical. You are now negotiating. It is simple enough to shut up and listen and think and yet few people feel naturally comfortable with silence. In negotiation you will need to stop and pause and think things through, whilst exercising patience. If it feels uncomfortable, it is; because you are now negotiating.

## PERSONAL VALUES

Values such as fairness, integrity, honesty and trust naturally encourage us to be open. Values can influence judgement, distort objectivity and lead to individuals compromising on otherwise strong commercial agreements. But the assumption that the longevity of relationships is dependent on cooperation is a common misconception. Personal values have their place within any relationship but business relationships can and often do exist, based on different value sets.

Values are usually deep-rooted and many people feel very defensive about them, as if their very integrity was being challenged. The point here is that they are not right or wrong. I am not suggesting that effective negotiators have no values – we all do. However, in negotiation, when you are involved in a process, what you *do* and what you *are* need not be the same thing. This is not about challenging who you are, but it is about helping you to change the things you *do*.

If you want to remain loyal to your values during negotiation there is nothing wrong with this. Others may not be as faithful to theirs, which could leave you compromised. In other words, if you choose to be open and honest by, for example, sharing information with the other party and they decide not to reciprocate, guess who will gain the balance of power? And how appropriate is that?

Where natural economic laws, such as supply and demand, result in people doing business with each other, a cooperative relationship can help to create greater opportunities but it is not always necessary. Trust and honesty are great corporate values: they are defendable and safe, especially when you have a business involving hundreds or thousands of people buying or selling on behalf of one business. They also help promote sustainable business relationships. However, in a negotiation, these values can be the root of complacency, familiarity and even lazy attitudes that end up costing shareholders money. At The Gap Partnership we remain strong believers in collaborative relationships but with the emphasis on optimizing value whilst ensuring the best interests of *all* involved.

## THE CASE FOR COLLABORATION

If you prefer collaborative negotiations it could be because:

- you need the commitment and motivation of the other party in order to deliver on what you have agreed;

- you prefer to work within a range of variables that allow you to consider all of the implications and the total value in play;
- you regard it as a better way of managing relationships; or that
- you simply fear conflict and the potential negative consequences of the negotiation breaking down.

Whatever your reason, you should ensure that it is because it's more likely to meet *your objectives* rather than simply a style preference that provides for a comfortable environment. How appropriate this is depends on how honest you are with yourself about your motives and the benefits that collaboration will bring.

### HONESTY WITH YOURSELF

It is often difficult to work out how good a deal you really have secured following a negotiation. This would be far easier to work out if, when we reviewed our performance, self-justification was left out of the equation. Denial results in us simplifying and justifying what happened without facing the stark truth. Have you ever asked yourself: "If I had performed differently or taken different decisions, could I have secured a better deal?" It is easier to move on rather than reflect on our performance and consider the what and the why, and of course the resulting quality of the deal we finished up with. Learning something from each negotiation ensures that, where unplanned compromises have taken place, you take away some value from the experience. This requires honesty with yourself. The following four areas provide a useful frame of reference for review, and as preparation for your next negotiation.

## THE FOUR CHALLENGES WE FACE

### *Challenge 1 – This is all about you*

Negotiation is uncomfortable. It sometimes involves silence, threats and consequences that many find difficult environments to perform well in. If you are to perform well, you will need to accept responsibility for your actions and recognize the significant difference your performance can make to every agreement you are involved in.

The art of negotiation can be learnt and applied, but you must have the self-motivation for change and the ability to be flexible. This is not just about being tough or being prepared. It is firstly about being motivated by the prospect of creating value and profit from well-thought-through agreements. You should therefore recognize that your past performance is no indication of your future performance, especially since every negotiation is unique, like every basketball or football game.

So, the first challenge is you. It is *people* who negotiate; not machines, or companies. We all have prejudices, values, likes and dislikes, preferences, pressures, objectives and judgement, as will the other party in your negotiations. So one part of our journey will involve understanding why our greatest challenge in negotiation is ourselves and how, by nature, we see the world from our perspective rather than that of the other party.

The simple process of an exploratory meeting, patience and seeking to work *with* someone, rather than to assume and then impose ideas on that person, is key to understanding how others see the world and what their objectives are when both selling and negotiating. As an effective negotiator you need to be able to understand the dynamics of any situation from "inside" the other party's head. Exploration and planning of this type requires a proactive discipline.

## CASE STUDY

Recently, one of our consultants was advising an account manager who was managing a US retailer. The account manager had attended a meeting with the retailer to present their company's latest investment strategy, which was to help deliver greater potential for profit. In effect, they were prepared to "invest" more money in the retailer in return for more space on the retailer's shelves and more promotions of their products. The investment proposition was financially strong, the numbers stacked up and the plan presented (to grow volume and mutual profitability) was well thought through. The problem was that the plan and the proposal had been created from inside the head of the branded manufacturing company based on what they wanted to achieve (more sales of their products) and not with their customer's current priorities in mind. They assumed that their customer's priority was increased profit, which was fair given that for years it was all they would want to talk about. However, changing market conditions had resulted in the retailer re-prioritizing what was important in order to compete. The presentation was cut short and the expected negotiation to follow never even got under way. The retailer had already decided to reduce the number of suppliers they sourced from and were interested only in how the supplier could help them compete with other discount retailers who were growing market share at an alarming rate.

### *Challenge 2 – There are no rules*

In negotiation there are no rules. No set procedures, no cans or cannots. Negotiation is often likened to a game of chess. The real difference is that in most negotiations you are not necessarily trying to beat an opponent, and are not restricted to alternate moves, as you are in chess.

Although there may be no absolute rules there are parameters within which we can operate. Most negotiators are empowered by their boss to negotiate but only to a certain level, beyond which discussions are usually escalated. Total empowerment results in exposure and danger because there are no parameters to protect us.

### *Challenge 3 – Knowing when you have performed well*

How will you know how well you have negotiated? You won't, because the other party is highly unlikely to tell you how you might have done better or how well you performed relative to their other options. It cannot simply be measured by "winning"; it's about the degree to which you have maximized the total value or opportunity. It might help to think of things relatively, based on where you have moved from on previous agreements, or to consider the market (how customers or suppliers are performing). However, if every situation is unique it is extremely difficult to gain an objective basis for measuring your performance against what might or what could have been. Every issue you negotiate will count and every variable that can affect the total value of your agreement needs to be included in your negotiation. Measuring your performance is always relative. It will also be about the degree to which the contract is honored or performed against. It can also be about whether the assumed value of the deal is ever fully delivered: even after you have signed the deal this measure remains unavailable.

So without the benefit of feedback from those we negotiate with, we have to rely on previous precedents (the outcome last time round), or absolute measurements (our profit and loss sheet), and have the humility to face such questions as:

- What might I have done differently?
- Might I have timed things differently?
- Might I have included other issues?
- Might I have tabled better thought-through proposals?
- Might I have not agreed so easily at the end?

Questions like these challenge how honest we are being with ourselves. A good deal has to be defined, taking all of the circumstances into account. Our ego can lead us to blame our circumstances when things go badly, and praise our performance when we think we have done well. By the time a deal is done, many of us just want to get on with implementation rather than reflect on our performance. Even if we know it's not a great deal but one that we can live with, many will find excuses such as:

- "It's better than having no deal at all."
- "It was worth it just to know that it will be done before the year-end."
- "We had no options, so took the offer so that we could move on to other things."
- "Better now than later."
- "It would only have depreciated in value had I not sold now."
- "We took our competitors out."

Measuring the quality of your agreement, without acknowledging some of the risks or concessions that were made that have allowed for **the price** to appear like a "good deal," is not measuring the total value, thus providing a true reflection of your performance. It is our honesty in self-review that needs to be encouraged if we are to truly measure the real value of our deals and learn from our performances.

**the price**
A single issue which offers but one measure and is usually not representative of the quality or total value or the agreement.

### No good, bad, right or wrong

In negotiation there is no good or bad, right or wrong. The economies we work in are dynamic as are our suppliers, customers and competitors. What was a great deal last week may be less well celebrated this week because our circumstances are continually changing. How well you negotiate will be measured by the outcome of your agreements. So negotiation is about doing things which are appropriate to each situation you face with the information as you see it at that moment in time. A better deal may simply be one that:

- recognizes and accounts for change in the future;
- carries less risk or a shorter tie-in period;
- has a lower deposit or even a high specification.

This need not mean simply a better price. Even a better price may not be good or bad. It simply depends on the whole package and the way you pull this together.

### Appropriateness

Knowing how a car was built and how it works does not make you a good driver. When driving with so many obstacles on the road, the challenge is to be able to maintain confidence, navigate, interpret and, where necessary, respond to situations in the most appropriate way when there is no absolute answer which suits all situations.

The same applies to negotiation in business.

- Should you set out to compete or to work with the other party?
- Should you seek to manipulate the situation or collaborate instead?
- Should you trust them or work on being trusted by them?
- How will your options influence the balance of power?
- Is the perception of power and dependency between you and the other party based on reality?

In so many cases the answer is based on *appropriateness*; that is, the ability to adapt and respond, depending on your circumstances. This requires an objective, rational, balanced mindset: a state that few human beings can maintain at all times, especially when faced with degrees of perceived conflict, rejection, and demands, all of which need to be accommodated within the negotiation. So what does this mean for you?

Appropriateness can relate to your behavior, the timing, the agenda you use, the people you involve and the options you introduce. It can relate to any stage of your negotiation.

For example, starting an annual price increase negotiation with a customer in December may be inappropriate given that the change comes into effect from January. Perhaps October would have been more appropriate. However, if your customer advises you in October that they are putting the contract up for re-tender and that you have been invited to enter a competitive tender process just to remain a supplier, it may prove inappropriate at that time to start positioning for a price increase. So the various circumstances that you face require you to weigh up the appropriate action required at that time.

The appropriate mindset to adopt in negotiation should be based on your own motivation and attitude. The motivation to perform has to come from a desire to maximize opportunity and value. Whether that includes cooperation or not (based on appropriateness), it is about managing the feelings, performance and position of the other party and there are many ways of achieving this, depending on your circumstances.

### *Challenge 4 – Nothing happens by accident*

The essence of negotiation is doing what is appropriate for your circumstances. This means being conscious of everything which happens before, during and after your negotiation, because in negotiation nothing happens by accident; everything happens for a reason. Being in control of yourself, your emotions and the relationship is a critical attribute for a negotiator. The challenge is that these qualities do not, for most of us, come naturally. Negotiators need to develop their awareness to the point that they do not lose touch with the human sensitivities necessary to manage relationships and that they do not compromise, for the sake of personal gratification that is for their own comfort, or to remove the stress they feel surrounding the consequences of deadlock.

## CONCLUSION

In summary, *The Negotiation Book* is about you. What I hope to provide is a thought-provoking insight into the reality of what it will take for you to become the Complete Skilled Negotiator. The more you understand tactics, strategies, behaviors, processes and planning tools, the better prepared you can become. Ultimately it is you, and perhaps your team, who will conduct your negotiations, you who will be accountable for your actions and the outcomes and you who may or may not act on the opportunities before you. It is you who will need to manage your relationships, emotions and the climate which so heavily influences possibility. If you have the nerve, the confidence, the courage and the motivation to change, I will remove the blindfold and share with you the amazing realities that can help you become a highly effective and creative negotiator with other people.

# CHAPTER 2

# The Negotiation Clock Face

The origin of the clock face and the framework of fourteen negotiation behaviors which supports it were born out of a commercial project I undertook in 1996. The project involved defining what is meant by "world class negotiation." My studies involved examining the many philosophies being advocated by gurus, universities, authors, consultancies and, importantly, the group of companies which I worked for at that time. In the main, I concluded that the approaches being taught by "experts" in the field were mainly one dimensional.

**win–win**
This is a term used to describe interest-based negotiations involving the low-cost, high-value trading exchange resulting in both parties gaining more from the trading process.

The first, a highly-rated academic institution, would preach that **win–win** was the rational and sustainable way of negotiating agreements, but without alternatives should this not work. The second, a consulting firm, promoted the highly ethical **partnership approach**, again with full rationale and justification for their recommendations.

**partnership approach**
This involves both parties sharing in risk taking, investment and potential, leaving both parties exposed to the risk and benefits associated with the trading relationship.

**"hard as nails" or hard bargaining**
These are terms used to describe win–lose negotiations involving aggressive positioning, tough tactics which serve to exploit any weakness in the other party's position which are in your short-term favor.

I was convinced by both of the arguments. I then attended a programme based on **"hard as nails"** negotiations. This is effectively how to **hard bargain**, negotiating with high levels of conflict, assumed power, and heavily reliant on positioning and manipulating the other party into accepting your offer. The approach had some merit but by now I was becoming confused in that each method promoted a one-way, one-dimensional approach as if to suggest that there was a "best" way of negotiating in all situations. Each approach, whether hard bargaining, win–win, partnership negotiations or **bidding and tendering process** negotiations, although in their own right plausible, assumed too much about how time, circumstance and the balance of power play their part in determining how one sets out to negotiate the "best outcome." Over the next two years I attended over a dozen negotiation programs across the US and Europe assessing the approaches and assumptions that underpinned them. Having read over 30 books on the subject covering everything from game-plan theory to linking and sequencing strategies, I found that most of them provided either very simplistic tactical approaches or complex explanations, which offered little by way of help to most people involved in practical negotiations.

**bidding and tendering process**
This is where market pressures are used to create competition within a controlled process. The effect is that the competitiveness of those involved helps to establish the true market value of that being sought.

## MAKING SENSE OF NEGOTIATION SO THAT WE CAN ALL BENEFIT FROM IT

To make sense of how different approaches to negotiation could serve us, and because of the unique challenges we all face, I developed a model called the Negotiation Clock Face.

The definitions used on the right-hand side of the clock face represent competitive negotiations based on those involved distributing a finite amount of value between them. This means that those on the right are tougher to negotiate in nature: what I get, you lose and what you get, I lose. So the process is going to be positional and potentially confrontational. The pie is only so big and it's simply a case of how it gets distributed.

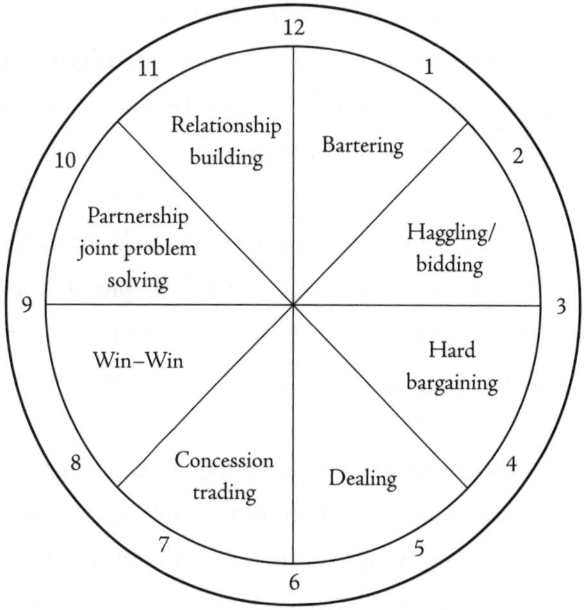


**Figure 2.1** The clock face.

Those definitions on the left-hand side of the clock face provide for more cooperation where collaborative negotiations lead to the creation of incremental value (creating a bigger pie). The definitions used here reflect those negotiations which are more commonly promoted in business-to-business situations, but not always. Between 6 and 12 o'clock there tends to be a broader range of issues used as part of building, engineering and negotiating agreements.

However, these definitions are only a guide in that many negotiations move from one area to another in the same meeting. For example, many partnership-based negotiations work well during the process, building ideas and trade-offs that result in the agreement becoming more valuable and more likely. At 8 o'clock, a simple trade-off between payment terms and volume can help both sides realize more value from an agreement. Although it is not uncommon to see two parties become ever more positional as the deal comes to a conclusion and the focus shifts to how the incremental value created is to be shared. For example,

> *"We have increased our volume order by 25% and we recognize the additional 2% discount that you have offered in return. However, if you want to maintain the historical four weeks order time, we will now require the higher quality packaging otherwise the deal is off."*

The value of the higher quality packaging is equivalent to a further 2% in value. Nothing is being offered in return for it, only a continuation of current terms relating to order times. A threat or consequence has now been tabled with it. What will follow is a cooling in the climate as the negotiation slips around to 4 or 5 o'clock where value is simply distributed. **The Complete Skilled Negotiator** would recognize this and manage the deal into the area that suits the situation, depending on those considerations which are important to them (relationship, sustainability or, if they choose, short-term value).

**the complete skilled negotiator**
This is a holistic term which relates to: behaviors, tactics, self-awareness, psychology, commercial acumen, adaptability, core traits, and more.

### *The "engineering of variables"*

The opportunity to build value through the "engineering of variables" and each party's relationships with the other is more likely to take place where there is collaboration in play, i.e. on the left-hand side of the clock. Collaboration of course requires some degree of common purpose, interest or dependency between those involved, as well as an appropriate environment. No matter how proactive or committed you are to developing a joint agreement, creating more value opportunities through negotiation requires the commitment of both parties, or such power on one side that the other has no option but to collaborate. Maximizing value through the engineering of variables need not be detrimental to the other party. They remain responsible for their actions and decisions as you remain responsible for yours. However, you should never allow complacency or the notion of fairness to affect your drive for improved terms as you will inevitably face resistance and challenge along the way however you build your agreements.

## SO WHO IS "THE COMPLETE SKILLED NEGOTIATOR"?

The Complete Skilled Negotiator is an individual who either possesses, or is conscious of those skills, attributes and attitudes necessary to negotiate effectively at any point on the clock face. They are balanced in their thinking, have their ego in check and are focused on understanding the interests and priorities of the other party. They are chameleon-like in their approach, in that they know how to be what they need to be depending on their circumstances and are not burdened by personal values which wear away at their consciousness. Their ability to read situations, take the time to prepare and have the capacity to think around the issues, as well as deal with the relationship dynamics at the same time, helps them perform in a confident manner. Most of all, they focus on the potential of the deal rather than trying to win, understanding that being competitive will only serve to attract friction which is generally counterproductive (unless used for a specific purpose).

The clock face is a model for helping you, the Complete Skilled Negotiator, to determine "appropriateness." It is defined by capitalism and reflects how people behave when negotiating. This provides for a conscious approach to negotiation which helps you manage the fear, the ambiguity, the greed and the egos involved. It also helps you to create value proactively, wherever available, in the most competitive arena in the world: the business market. Appropriateness simply allows us to interpret the many market and relationship conditions we face and respond accordingly.

The clock face model is not good or bad, right or wrong, any more than north, south, east or west is the right direction for any journey. It just "is" and wherever capitalism exists the clock face serves to offer a simple range of definitions within which your negotiations will take place. It is important to remember that the direction you take, decisions you make, performance you offer and results you achieve still remain *your* responsibility. The clock face is simply a compass.

## THE THREE FACTORS THAT INFLUENCE EVERY NEGOTIATION

### *1. Power*

Even if you conclude that the other party needs this deal more than you, their ego could still prevent them from agreeing. There are many who walk away from the table, even though the deal on offer is better than any other option they have, because they feel manipulated. Often their ego will not allow them to give you the satisfaction of winning or, sometimes, if it's regarded as unfair in their minds, they will even walk and pay more elsewhere. This is not rational, it's emotional, but it is people we negotiate with and their emotions that we need to take into account. Power does not give you the right to manipulate. To understand power in negotiation is one thing, to understand how to apply it to achieve your objectives is another.

#### Managing your options

The level of dependency between two parties is heavily influenced by options (supply and demand) and by whatever time and circumstance means to those involved. If you have no options and need to secure an agreement you have a low level of power, assuming of course that the other party knows this. Now, if they have no idea of the number of options you have it may make no difference unless you are busy weighing up the situation in your own head and allow yourself to believe you have little or no power. What if they have no options and are in equal need of an agreement? Who has the balance of power now? And what of the implications of time? Let's say that they need to secure your services within a few days, without which they will face other implications. It could be that even with no options available to you, you are still in a more powerful position than they are. This is of course dependent on you establishing this. Where time and circumstances are concerned, knowledge and information offer power. If you are unaware of the other party's circumstances you will not be able to negotiate effectively because the only circumstances you will understand will be your own.

Make it your business to understand their business and be inside their head.

### *2. Trust*

To work towards an agreement you need some form of cooperation. Most people prefer to do business with people they understand and can trust. Most experienced negotiators, whether from banks, oil companies, even governments, recognize the importance of building trust and some level of mutual understanding. Building a common business agenda promotes a common focus and acceptance which leads to greater opportunities in developing a successful agreement together. It encourages open dialogue, willingness and creative thinking born out of the mutual desire to build trust through cooperation.

Of course not all deals are conducted in this way. Nor is trust compulsory. However, if you are able to maintain a good balance between trust and respect, and create the right environment in your meetings, you will have created an environment where it's possible to secure better and more sustainable agreements. It is important not to confuse respect and trust with the notion of being liked. People who have an inherent need to be liked are more likely to concede or not hold tough on a position simply because they feel that by doing so they will offend the other party. The ability to be diplomatic and to manage any tension in the situation is critical to being an effective negotiator.

**CASE STUDY**

A client of The Gap Partnership owned two Range Rovers. In 2009, during the UK recession, both cars were taken to a dealership at the same time for servicing. The dealership was having a tough time. Range Rovers were not selling and many customers were sending their cars to cheaper garages for servicing. When the dealership returned the serviced cars, the client found that they had added extra charges without consultation for the disposal of oil, and for providing and charging for spare oil which they had not requested, or been previously advised of. The client challenged the dealership who subsequently agreed to refund the amount as a credit the next time the cars were serviced. It was the last time my client dealt with the garage. This short-term gain attempted by the dealership damaged their customer's trust in them and the relationship ceased. It turned out to be a rather expensive way of making a quick £60, as the client purchased two replacement cars from a different dealership just 12 months later.

### Breaking trust

Building trust in business takes time and cannot be expected from the outset. It is based on an understanding which more commonly develops where there is some mutual dependency and need for an ongoing relationship. However, when one party takes advantage of the relationship the trust can quickly dissolve, as can the sustainability of the relationship and the business which depends on this. This can happen at any level of business (see case study above).

## CASE STUDY

Negotiation features throughout our lives and it is not exclusive to business. It was the morning of the first Sunday of December and my wife asked me at short notice to take the family to buy a Christmas tree. A trip to our local garden centre would have been followed by the task of loading the tree onto the car, getting it home, setting it up and dressing it with lights and decorations. I had already planned to spend the day writing this book and suggested an alternative (next weekend) to buy the tree, reassuring my wife that we had plenty of time, and that I needed to start writing my book. My wife conceded and I "won," or so I thought. Goodwill in the family for the day deteriorated. The kids wouldn't talk to me and conditions were placed that we would have to buy a different, even more expensive tree. I started to weigh up the cost of the three hours I had just "won." Had I really won or might there have been a better solution? Should I have involved the kids in the conversation? Those of you who have negotiated with children will know how difficult and uncompromising this can be. Or could I have secured more time and support from my wife in return for a more flexible attitude towards the family's needs? For me it highlighted how some creative thinking might have led to a more mutually beneficial solution. Finding ways to say "yes" in such a way that you can still achieve what you need to achieve (and often more) provides a healthy mindset for any negotiator.

### *3. Understanding total value and mutual opportunities*

There are many opportunities worth considering during an agreement that can be too quickly overlooked. These can include: future orders, volume, payment, delivery scheduling, specification, longer-term agreements, exclusivity opportunities, performance benefits and so on. The more issues up for negotiation, the more scope there is to grow the total value of the agreement. The greater the number of issues, the more possibilities available to negotiate around.

Total value, which includes all forms of risk, should be factored into your planning. For example, a garden centre placing an order for garden furniture will be keen to ensure that delivery timescales, order times, quality assurance and packaging are all featured highly on the agenda. There is no point in getting a great price on furniture that arrives too late in the season or that you can't deliver to your customers in good time. Because of size and weight, the costs associated with sending returns back to the manufacturer as a result of damage or poor quality is high, so these and other issues, which reflect the total supply cost, have to be included in your total value considerations.

## WHY ARE THERE SO MANY DIFFERENT WAYS TO NEGOTIATE A DEAL?

Capitalism and market pressures motivate and manipulate people to operate in the ways that they do. For example, account managers frequently become frustrated when trying to build relationships with buyers who they perceive to have more power within the relationship. The buyer (and this often works both ways) will negotiate competitively to drive every last cent of value out of the deal. As a result the buyer can become so focused on one issue that they are prepared to forfeit any other benefits whilst in the pursuit of the best price. Meanwhile, the account manager, desperate to build value through a range of variables (payment terms, volume, quality, delivery and other offerings), tries to progress conversations on a collaborative basis resulting in proposals which in this case go ignored.

So what is the answer? There is no one answer. How you negotiate will nearly always depend on the specific circumstances you face. This is why, to understand negotiation, you first need a basis for differentiating the many ways in which negotiation can and does take place (the Negotiation Clock Face). The above situation however is certainly manageable. Escalation to a higher authority, introducing more items onto the agenda, conditional movement from your position or even introducing time constraints could offer a start.

When asked to describe their preferred negotiation style, many negotiators will openly talk about how they get the best results, the way that best suits their industry or the way their business does business. The response is rarely "it depends." The importance of relationships will often feature as the primary motive for preferring collaborative negotiations. This view of how negotiations can best be managed usually results in the individuals being effective in only one type of negotiation or relationship situation. The Complete Skilled Negotiator has a much broader understanding of the options available and is able to effectively adjust to each situation as they find it.

### *There is no right or wrong in negotiation*

We must understand the jungle we operate in; what it is that capitalism does to influence the way value is distributed or created. If capitalism is the market and the level of dependency we have in a relationship acts like a tide pulling us in or pushing us out, then we need a point of reference to help us differentiate and define the appropriate approach for any situation, which is where the usefulness of the Negotiation Clock Face comes to the fore.

Another way of defining the point of "appropriateness" is "fit for purpose." Do the behaviors, skills and tactics associated with hard bargaining meet the needs of a negotiator involved in buying a second-hand car? The answer is: it depends. If financing, availability, payment terms are variables for example, it may be worth adopting a slightly less aggressive dealing stance. If price is the only factor, and there is no relationship or a need for one, in such cases hard bargaining may be appropriate to your objectives.

## HOW THE NEGOTIATION CLOCK FACE WORKS

The Negotiation Clock Face offers a visual representation of negotiation styles ranging from the toughest form of market manipulation through to high dependency relationships. Each stage around the clock face offers more complexity, more opportunity and more collaboration required. It helps us to understand and determine the most appropriate approach to negotiate, depending on your circumstances.

The clock face as a reference point, therefore, helps you to consciously adopt the appropriate approach related to what you are trying to achieve and the circumstances you face. It is not designed to be prescriptive nor does it suggest that your negotiation should take place at one particular point of the clock face. Many negotiations fluctuate depending on what stage the negotiation is at. The clock face, therefore, is not a process suggesting that you should start at one point and move sequentially to another, it is simply a model which highlights the different styles of negotiation available to us.

*The negotiation environment*

If we are going to control any negotiation we have to first understand the environment within which we operate. For example, imagine you are responsible for managing a particular customer on an ongoing basis. You feel that a relationship is going to serve your long-term interests, which requires you to build some level of trust and an understanding with your customer. However, your customer has significant market power and exerts pressure on you to improve your terms. This makes your relationship difficult and transactional in nature as their behavior suggests their interests are in short-term gains only.

Do you choose to spend your time at 4 o'clock hard bargaining and risk suboptimizing longer-term opportunities (ignoring other possible variables) or do you attempt to move them around to 10 o'clock to work on the relationship in an attempt to gain a more mutually beneficial solution?

The answer to this again is "it depends." So by understanding the different factors that can influence your negotiations, you can build a stronger awareness of whether you need to proactively change the nature of your relationship with the other party and/or the climate of your meetings during your negotiations.

The skills and attitudes required to negotiate at a different point of the clock face differ. In principle the left-hand side of the clock face (6–12 o'clock) illustrates those negotiations where there is more dependency, higher levels of trust and a broader agenda around which to negotiate value. In contrast, the right-hand side symbolizes transactional negotiations, with lower levels of trust and fewer issues regarded as important enough to negotiate. All the definitions on the right-hand side of the clock face are either win–lose or competitive forms of negotiation.

### *Bartering: 1 o'clock*

Bartering involves the art of trading one thing off against another and does not necessarily involve money. Trade bartering has taken place around the world for thousands of years before money even existed. Today there are websites dedicated to bartering or "swapping."

**CASE STUDY**

In 2005 the US entrepreneur Kyle MacDonald started with a paperclip and swapped (traded) this up in 14 steps to a house a year later.

Price bartering, as anyone who has ever bought that carpet at the Egyptian market stall will know, can be very quick and the final process can be far removed from the market value. Our satisfaction is from having secured the carpet for only $XX when back home it would have cost $YY, regardless of the implications of getting it home or even whether we needed one at all. Both the culture and rituals employed in the Middle East make this form of negotiation process "normal" and comfortable for locals. There is a ritual, a process to go through where we establish the value of something between us. Indeed it is usual for locals to insist on getting to know each other before business can even be discussed. It's common for entire families to be involved in this process. It's how business is done: it involves trust, personality and yes, capitalism. It is a process they are far more comfortable with than those conditioned differently in Western cultures.

How much the person you are negotiating with needs to sell and how much you want to buy will effectively determine the price within your own micro-market place of supply and demand. There need not be any relationship, trust or even respect, simply a ritual to agree on the price. When bartering, the parties try to pretend that there is respect or trust in what each other is saying. At least when we move around to 3 and 4 o'clock there may not be much trust but there is enough integrity in place that the pretending has stopped. However, when it comes down to conducting business, this is the rawest form of capitalism: how much you want something and how much I need to trade something within our own micro economy. Nothing else matters. In negotiation terms it's raw, basic and yet effective. It's at 1 o'clock because it represents about as basic a form of negotiation as you can get. Until money was invented it was the only way to negotiate of material value.

### *Bidding: 2–3 o'clock*

Websites such as eBay have helped create new industries in the way products and services are traded around the world. The days of the sleepy antique auctions, although still in operation, have been taken over by a vast online bidding industry. Today you can trade almost anything online via designated business auction traders or business to consumer (B2C) sites. Even the stock market operates using the process of bidding where ultimately the market (supply and demand) will define the value of the transaction.

Yet, as companies continue to seek ways of buying commodity-based products on the best terms, the bidding process is here to stay. Where there are a healthy number of suppliers willing to compete for the business, the opportunity to use online bidding processes continues to deliver the best possible prices. Such is the control and power that bidding processes provide that private equity backed Swoopo, at least until March 2011, used to charge you (and they had over 1.2 million customers) for each bid you made. As you can imagine, this encouraged bidders who bid early on in the process to continue with their bidding. Having paid to bid, they had fallen victim to what economists call the **sunk cost fallacy**. They say that Swoopo used to make as much money from its charges for bidding as it did on the products offered. This means that even if the winning bid is a low one, providing there have been enough bids, Swoopo's management of the process ensured the business was profitable, or so their private equity backers believed. In March 2011 the company filed for bankruptcy in Germany. The process used, however, is very dangerous, very controlling, and with enough players involved, very disempowering.

**sunk cost fallacy**
Sunk costs are retrospective (past) costs that have already been incurred and cannot be recovered. Sunk costs are sometimes contrasted with prospective costs, which are future costs that may be incurred or changed if an action is taken.

This basic means of agreeing a price demands the greatest of all self-disciplines: being prepared to walk away. The risks of becoming too competitive with no alternative options before entering into a bidding war are well illustrated by the government sell-off of the 3G mobile phone licences in the UK during 2000. The mobile phone operators ended up paying many times the value for the privilege of gaining one of the four licences up for auction. You may have thought that these multi-billion pound businesses would have used sales projections and profit forecasts to work out the limits beyond which they could not go. The other consideration was that there could only be four winners and these were going to be the players who would be around to compete in the future. The others won't be able to compete. So the limits the companies were prepared to pay became greater than the commercial reality suggested at the time. The "winners" ended up paying £22.5 billion in what became the biggest auction of its kind in modern business. It took a further eight years before 3G technology took hold of the market and financial returns could start to be realized.

**tendering processes** . An invitation to tender for the contract by submitting your best proposal against a briefing document. The organizers of the process use this as a means of narrowing down a shortlist or even selecting the winners of the contract.

Businesses that use **tendering processes** are effectively using the bidding process to attract a price-based best offer from a range of potential suppliers. Local government contracts widely use this process for subcontracting purposes as part of the procurement process to ensure that competitive pressures are maintained and that tax payers are getting good value. However, where the nature of the contract is based on a performance-related service, for example the building of a road, price alone, even against a well-specified brief can prove a restrictive means of agreeing all terms and can lead to poor "total value" agreements. However, without such transparent competitive procedures, government procurement would be more susceptible to illegal forms of bribery.

Many businesses use the 2–3 o'clock approach (Haggling and Bidding) and build in a post-tender negotiation process with those who have effectively qualified to the final stage of potential suppliers. This allows the negotiation to move around the clock face to a win–win situation at 8 o'clock or beyond, providing for greater synergies to be realized.

### *Hard bargaining: 4 o'clock*

Hard bargaining in its purest form is not typically the preferred approach in business-to-business negotiations, but even complex negotiations such as those which involve the acquisition of companies frequently move to 4 o'clock on the final issues. This is typically when all the remaining issues have been exhausted and one final issue remains unresolved. It is under these pressured conditions when the skill, mindset and confidence to hard bargain is both necessary and critical.

#### "What I get, you lose, and what you get, I lose"

For those of us who believe in fairness, hard bargaining provides the greatest of tests. It is not fair, it is uncomfortable, it requires nerve and it will make you question whether the discomfort was worth the benefit which came from it. Your opening position is likely to be rejected (if not it would have been inappropriate) and you are likely to be facing someone who is trying to understand how far you will go.

Of course hard bargaining for yourself is a different experience from doing it on behalf of the company you work for. Although it may not be your preferred approach to negotiation, it has to be understood in order to avoid leaving yourself vulnerable. Where

**bargaining range**

The bargaining range is the difference between the most you will pay and the least the other party will accept.

people or companies have power, they will use it to their commercial benefit and if you are not equipped to perform under such circumstances you will pay more than you need to.

The two most important disciplines in any negotiation consist of asking questions and making proposals. Information is power and at 4 o'clock, power will play a part in how the **bargaining range** is divided. This is rarely transparent. If you told the other party what your breakpoint was (your bottom line), would they be prepared to pay a cent more?

The art of hard bargaining is of course to work out what *their* breakpoint is – that is, negotiate from inside their head.

Once you understand their interests, priorities, time pressures and options, you will be better positioned to be able to gauge how far and hard you can push. One assumes that the other party is responsible

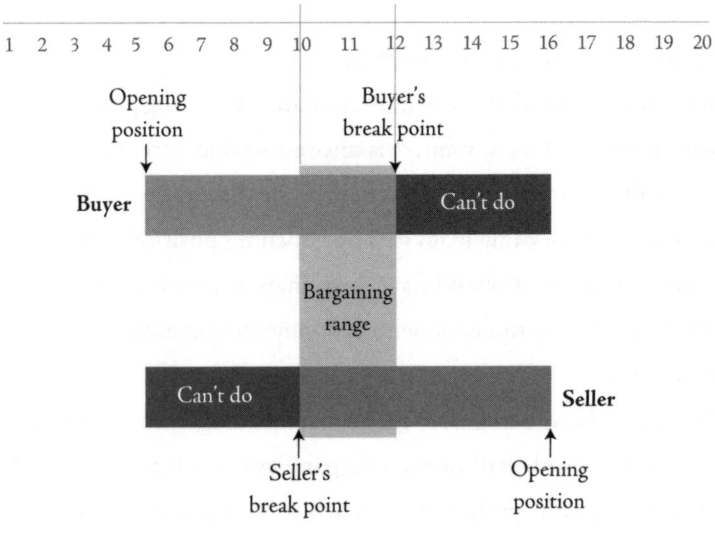


**Figure 2.2** Hard bargaining positioning.

for their own interests. They are unlikely to agree to anything they cannot or don't want to agree to. Your questions will provide you with ever more forms of information and as a result help make your position more powerful. If you are not asking questions you should be making a proposal by stating them. On the other hand, if you are faced with a skilled hard bargainer who has adopted a silent stance and an extreme position of their own, you must be prepared to hold firm, be patient and reiterate your position.

### Delivering a proposal

When stating your proposal, you should set out to create an anchor from which the other person feels that they need to reassess their own expectations. It should be extreme and yet realistic. Too extreme and they may just walk away from any further dialogue. Your opening position is simply the start of a process during which you set out to manage their expectations. Most start out in negotiations with expectations of what they want to achieve and the first step towards shifting expectation is to provide a figure or position which you know to be unacceptable but is not so extreme that they walk away. Once you have set this position you have started the process of shifting their expectations by placing an anchor in place. Everything becomes relative to this position, even your concessions, in that you know you will have to move if a deal is to be agreed. Yes, they are going to reject it so get used to the word "no." Yes, they will be emotional as they express their shock and surprise. This is to be expected and is all part of the process. However, if you antagonize or insult the other party, for example by opening at too extreme a position, you risk losing the chance of maintaining a conversation and ultimately completing the deal, even if you have significant power. So the art of hard bargaining is gauging your opening position and then being tough on issues like price, whilst remaining respectful of the people you are negotiating with. This means:

- appropriate positioning;
- holding tough; and
- conceding on fewer occasions and by lesser amounts than the other party.

In the majority of cases, negotiators who make their offer first will come out ahead.

Another characteristic of hard bargaining anchoring consists of stating a position as a fact early in the dialogue. It can be one of the most powerful tactics available to you for gaining psychological power. In situations where there are no clear market value indicators and there is scope for the perception of value to be different from market value, first offers have an incredibly strong anchoring effect.

This relative positioning of what I call "playing at home" exerts a strong pull throughout the rest of the negotiation as counter-offers and moves become relative to the opening anchoring position (your home position). If you start playing away it means that you are trying to move them from their position and once you start to do this you are more likely to finish up closer to their position than to yours. Of course, this is much easier to control if you have a level of real transparent power. For example it's pretty easy to look confident in a game of poker if you have four aces, but less so with two 3s.

Medium- or long-term positioning can be more subtle. It can occur over weeks, months or even years, perhaps making the same statement in different ways over many interactions. The statement may firm up as the negotiation approaches, or may be delivered again and again, with the negotiation only occurring when the negotiator deems the anchoring positioning to have created the right conditions and timing for success, more likely.

### Performance

To perform as a hard bargainer you need to maintain self-control, to shut up and listen. You will be amazed how many people find the very basic discipline of asking questions, making proposals and then shutting up impossible to perform when under pressure. Most of us are conditioned as "warm and sociable" people who have business ethics that include a need for sustainable business relationships. However, with the need to be liked, we run the risk of talking, justifying and eventually conceding unnecessarily when the going gets tough. The challenge with mastering hard bargaining is to put your personal needs to one side and recognize the need to adopt a process which is fit for purpose and to do so through strong self-discipline, self-awareness and acceptance of the gamesmanship in play.

## *Dealing: 5–6 o'clock*

The timing of the contract (the sooner the contract can be completed) may have as much benefit to me as it has a downside to you: bonus payments may be as costly for you to achieve as they are for me to provide. So although each agenda item needs agreeing and perhaps even trading, they may not necessarily provide any incremental benefit. Where you are faced with simply agreeing on terms, which provide little by way of any real incremental benefit, a deal-like climate is likely to exist and the need to be considered, conditional and tough during your dealings is critical to you in protecting your position and the value of the deal.

The process of deal-making is usually made up of trade-offs and compromises rather than of low-cost, high-value trades as found in classic win–win situations. This is because where time pressures are in play and there is a need to make the deal work, trades tend to be made up of "necessary" moves to make the deal work rather than value-adding activity, although the two are not mutually exclusive.

Deal-making can involve few issues, which means the style and dialogue can sometimes be little more than hard bargaining, although the climate tends to be more respectful. The difference is that you can offer to move on one issue providing them with some satisfaction subject to a reciprocal move allowing for the deal to be completed. Price as we know is the most contentious and transparent of all variables which is why, when negotiated alone, it tends to lead to competitive forms of negotiation. When dealing is in play at 5–6 o'clock there can be three or four issues involved, each of which are transparent and, although they need agreeing, they provide little by way of opportunity for mutual gain.

### *Concession trading: 6–7 o'clock*

This is the first of the collaborative approaches where both parties recognize that some level of cooperation is required if mutual interests are to progress. The more common interests that can be identified amongst the two parties, the greater the potential for creating value. The process can involve conditional trade-offs across a broad range of issues from a pre-agreed agenda.

The negotiation climate is usually constructive but still guarded. For example, saying "if you place the order today, we will guarantee you your required time slot," would seem to be an offer to move things around to accommodate the other party. It could, however, be the case that you were going to do this anyway, that there is no cost implication in offering the time slot or that you have very few orders so they could have had any time slot without any implications to you. All that matters is that you were seen to offer a conditional concession (in this case, the condition that the order is placed today) and were providing some value (convenience and security of securing an important time slot), leaving the other party with the satisfaction that they have agreed a "*good deal*" with you.

Now that you are on the left-hand collaborative side of the clock face, your focus should be on working "on the deal." Nothing is agreed until everything is agreed, which means that you can park issues or variables and come back to them if not agreed on. An unresolved issue does not mean there is a deadlock but that other issues need to be examined in order to help resolve the current impasse.

So what are the negotiation variables that help create greater opportunity on the left-hand side of the clock face? Most negotiations from 7 o'clock onwards are made up of six fundamental variables: Price, Payment, Volume, Specification, Delivery and Contract Period. That is to say that most other variables will be a variant of, or will be in some way linked to, these six. It could be that you introduce a further forty variables which will in some way shape or form be related to these six. I have outlined a broader range of variables which are linked to these core six in Chapter 9.

### How does concession trading differ from win–win negotiations?

Often in business, managers try to form relationships where the balance of power is not even (one party needs the other more). One

**concession trading**
This is where the party with less power agrees to concede points to the other party in order to maintain the deal.

party will hard bargain, the other will be focused on agreeing a range of issues which are all interrelated. Sound familiar? For many organizations **concession trading** is a default position. This may not be ideal or how they would prefer to do business but the balance of power within the relationship means that without careful planning over the long term, leading to the naturalizing of dependency, concession trading is probably the best they can hope for. It's also frustrating, which is a further challenge for you. The essence of a good negotiator is the ability to handle frustration because the other party will rarely agree to your initial proposal.

### *Win–win: 8 o'clock*

Win–win implies by its very definition that both sides in a negotiation win or come out ahead. The rational process of trading low-cost, high-value issues in such a way that the total value opportunity can be enhanced was popularized in the 1980s in the book *Getting to Yes* by Ury and Fisher. The concept of win–win assumes that both parties will make decisions based on the fact that, if one party offers you something of greater value than that which they seek, in return leaving you with an incremental gain, then you are more likely to accept it. If your aim is to build value, it's difficult to argue with the theory. However, as Ury and Fisher later went on to write in *Beyond Reason*, the emotional side of a relationship plays a significant part in how agreements actually come together. People are not always rational in their behavior.

Later, the Program on Negotiation at Harvard (of which Ury and Fisher were members) went on to acknowledge that the process of negotiation was indeed a process of value creation followed by value

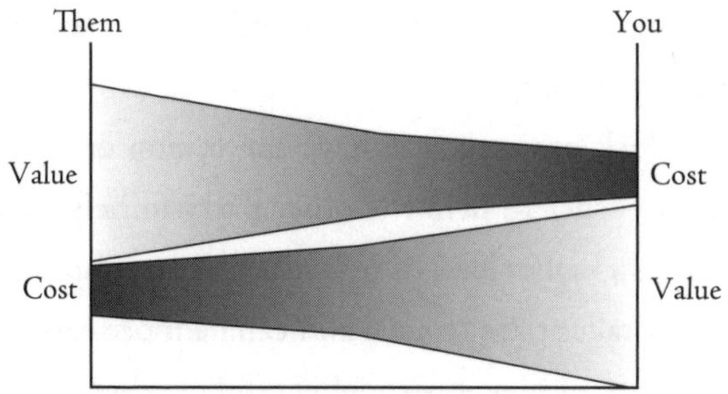


**Figure 2.3** Low cost high value win–win trade-offs.

distribution. So, even though two parties may work together to build value through low-cost, high-value trade-offs, each party would still employ their power to secure as much of the incremental value they jointly created for themselves. In theory, win–win involves lower levels of conflict and results in a better deal for both parties since it is based on collaborative efforts, but responsibility still remains on both sides to maximize the opportunities involved for their own business. The incremental value traded is rarely split 50:50 because most of the value associated with the issues traded are not transparent to both parties, so can shift quickly to tough value distribution based discussions. This is the equivalent of starting a negotiation at 8 o'clock and finishing it at 4 o'clock. This is not good or bad, just reflective of what often happens.

Win–win provides the opportunity to be creative with trade-offs, introducing issues such as the longevity of the agreement, the relative risks each party is prepared to take and often intangible issues such as convenience and flexibility. The value you place on any of these comes from the value you and the other party place on them. In the same way, if you remain guarded about the value you place on particular issues, you cannot expect the other party to simply come up with viable proposals.

From 8 o'clock onwards you have the option of sharing some information in order to help the other party to help you. This of course requires a higher level of trust than when simply concession trading. Trust takes time to earn and can be more easily nurtured when the balance of power is roughly even or when the dominant party has a genuine motive for securing your commitment to an agreement.

### *Problem solving: 9–10 o'clock*

When building an agenda for a 10 o'clock negotiation as a Complete Skilled Negotiator, your mindset should be focused on forming a sustainable agreement that covers all areas, including:

- performance
- compliance
- risk.

Take the concept of total value agreements that are central to win–win negotiations and extend the possibilities through building more dependency between parties. For instance, if this benefits us, it will benefit you; if it harms us, it will harm you. Focus your attention on what issues could create problems during the lifetime of the agreement for both parties. Take your time working through the level of risk and responsibilities that both of you are prepared to take. Then build an agreement which ensures that responsibility is transparent and clearly stated and that risk is clearly compensated for.

**CASE STUDY**

Graham was involved in selling his house in London and approached a local estate agent to market the property. The going rate for selling a house at the time was 2% of the sale price. The market was slow, it was a buyer's market but Graham had no option. He needed to sell for personal reasons. The estate agent conducted a survey and advised that the house should be marketed at £1.5 million for a quick sale. Graham was concerned about the financial implications of the house taking months to sell. His circumstances required him to sell within three months. As a negotiator he was tempted to negotiate the 2% fee down but instead recognized that it was in his interest to partner with his estate agent. He held a meeting and introduced a number of variables to the manager of the estate agent's office. He escalated the discussion to the manager's level to ensure that the decision-making authority would be able to respond to his proposal. He proposed that the estate agent received their 2%. In addition to this they would receive 20% of anything over the £1.5 million received subject to the house being sold within three months. The house was placed on the market at £1.75 million. Not only was the house sold within three months, it sold for £1.7 million. The additional £160,000 he received for his house was far in excess of anything he might have achieved by negotiating a reluctant discount on the fee.

Where there is an established relationship, contractual problems can, in some cases, even help to strengthen the agreement and also increase the value of the contract. Renegotiating terms to resolve issues provides the opportunity to reappraise circumstances. It allows for a fresh look at the agreement and risks can be renegotiated and the total value redistributed. Most deals have terms and conditions negotiated, which relate to the risks associated with the contract. Yet contractual terms can also provide positive incentives. For instance, bonuses in the event that parts of the work are completed within agreed time frames or shared consequences in the event that delivery commitments are not fulfilled as agreed.

### *Relationship building: 10–12 o'clock*

The value of partnership in business cannot be underestimated. It often represents the optimum position for building agreements when trading partners are interdependent and there is a clear need to help each other to realize the efficiencies, synergies and saving as part of how they work continuously together. It is an "ideal" situation and in some cases works but very often proves difficult to achieve and sustain. Why? Performance change and changes in the market result in an ever-shifting environment. Sometimes these changes have been factored into the agreement and sometimes they serve to expose one party or the other. At 10–12 o'clock, risks will have been considered as part of the original agreement. However, if one party suffers as a result of change that could result in the trading relationship being affected, both parties are more likely to reappraise the trading arrangement and sometimes even renegotiate the terms. The degree of interdependency in play means both parties are implicated if one is affected by change.

When negotiating past 10 o'clock your agenda should be designed to encourage transparency, creativity and possibility. In essence, the broader the agenda the greater the scope for building robust deals with added value. Examining longevity, intangibles (things which are not material), risk, sustainability, information, resources and so on allow for highly creative agreements to be built that reflect all of the interests, needs for flexibility and potential opportunities for both parties. But this ideal requires understanding and patience and in some cases an acceptance that the reduced risks achieved by longer-term agreements may have to come at the cost of short-term margin or profit maximization. If that is desirable then the partnership approach may well prove appropriate. Much will depend on the circumstances and objectives of those involved.

### Back to bartering

In Tim Harford's book *The Undercover Economist* he explains how the cost and value of a cup of coffee can vary and why the average commuter is prepared to pay a premium for a cup of coffee at the train station or airport when time is a premium and supply and demand are in favor of the well-positioned coffee kiosk. Although you may be a regular customer of the kiosk as you rush to the office, and may have become loyal to a particular brand of coffee as a result, your relationship is not a partnership. Indeed, the balance of power as a result of supply and demand is still firmly in favor of the strategically positioned coffee kiosk. Your ability and your motive to negotiate in public over a few cents is removed. Also, the kiosks with loyalty scheme cards effectively constitute a proposal made to their loyal customers: a retrospective discount, a loyalty incentive, more coffee rather than a lower price, a trade barter and low-cost, high-value incentive which takes us past 12 o'clock and back to where we started with Bartering.

### *Exploring the reality of partnerships*

Partnerships provide the necessary veneer enabling many agreements to be progressed in business – yet beneath there lies a charade. Some corporations believe so strongly in partnerships that their values and ethics strongly promote them through and across their business.

Ethical partnerships carry a sense of righteousness about them. Few companies would openly admit that they are out to screw every last cent out of their customers or suppliers and yet they are required to provide statements about maximizing shareholder value. Again this cannot always be achieved without someone else paying and the larger the organization, the more leverage they have for doing so. I am not suggesting that partnerships do not exist, but in all my experience in business they are rarely as idealistic or as reflective as the true definition of partnership might suggest. Formed partnerships take the form of unions, marriages, cooperatives, societies, confederations, alliances, associations, institutions and there are many more entities which are based on common interests, values and motives for investment. By their very nature, two or more businesses working together are going to be challenged – they will have independent interests to consider and you must always remain mindful and aware of these considerations.

Building value through partnerships requires dependency whilst using natural, competitive economic pressures to ultimately sustain the commitment to invest in the relationship, rather than to simply seek short-term gains. Knowing which relationship to compete in and which relationship to invest in should help inform you as to which part of the clock face to operate from.

Where partnerships do work is where the relationship is of *strategic* importance, i.e. where the businesses could easily be compromised if the relationship were not to "perform" and that the investment in time and effort delivers obvious mutual synergy benefits. Although partnerships perform better with trust, trust can take time to earn and requires the glue of dependency. Once it exists it can also be harmful in that it can serve to disarm, promoting familiarity and complacency. So a continued balancing act needs to be "policed" through measurement, performance reviews and sponsorship for the partnership to be sustainable. These considerations should feature early in the negotiation agenda as being critical to the sustainability of any agreement that you may build.

### What makes a strong partnership?

Many partnerships in business point to those who have worked on the same side. But the reality is that your business probably carries a relatively short-term view of performance. With shareholder pressure, obligations to perform, and information provided weekly, monthly and quarterly, the need to deliver a return on investment (ROI) results in a focus on deals which deliver value today.

Your customer or supplier informs you that they intend to cancel the contract, de-list the product, serve notice, and reduce the order or the range. When what once seemed safe and endless ceases, the questions come. In your dismay and confusion you ask yourself questions like:

- Why did they not talk to us?
- How did I not see this coming?
- Should I have invested more in the relationship?

You think it's too late or you find yourself clinging on from an apparently weaker position (although they may be posturing). You find yourself scrambling to save what you thought was safe. You suddenly realize that the partnership was little more than some convenient title they had offered up in return for more concessions from you. You had lost track of the commercial reality and why you thought the idea was a good one in the first place.

This may not be what you were expecting at the ultimate 12 o'clock position, but there are few partnerships that do not at some point extinguish themselves, or cease to exist beyond their useful life. In the real world there tends to be a dominant partner in the relationship. Even in marriage, different strengths emerge between husband and wife that influence the way decisions are made about different issues. Just consider the number of marriages that fail to last longer than five years.

### Partnerships have no place for comfort, familiarity or complacency

During my journeys to clients around the world, I find myself making my way through airports to or from the departure/arrival gates. Many airports are so vast that it can take 30 minutes to walk from the lounge area to your departure gate. Signs indicate walking times and moving walkways reduce the burden for thousands of passengers a day. One interesting observation I have made consistently is that when people step onto a moving walkway, they start to walk more slowly than they were before, or sometimes they just stop. The motion of the walkway makes the individual feel as though they are making good progress and therefore they don't have to work so hard at getting to their gate. In relative terms they are achieving as much but with less effort. Their personal productivity drops because they are now being "carried along" with no concern for those waiting behind them.

Partnerships, once formed, have been known to have a similar effect. They can promote complacency and familiarity and can be bad for business and ultimately the start of the end of the relationship. The partnership should be a basis for being even more productive.

Business relationships have to be earned and they need to pay for themselves. From a negotiation point of view, once the partnership has been formed, however formal or informal, the relationship and the incremental value available should become the focus of attention.

When seeking to build a B2B business relationship you need to form an understanding of where motives, dependencies, time frames and stakeholders' attitudes are. The prospect of achieving real synergy can only come from mutual benefit and this needs to be clear to all. Only then can the motivation to commit investment in time, effort and flexibility be realized, helping the relationship to build.

## SUMMARIZING THE NEGOTIATION CLOCK FACE

Love and hate are regarded to be emotions that are very close to each other and yet are opposites. So it is with the 12 o'clock and 1 o'clock positions on the Negotiation Clock Face. The challenge for you as a Complete Skilled Negotiator is to remain focused on the value involved in the deal and not on yourself. If you can exercise the patience to question and listen and treat others with respect you will not only build power through knowledge but you will secure a commitment to trade through the respect you offer being reciprocated. Channelling your emotional energy in the appropriate way will enable you to control where you are on the clock face rather than becoming a victim to the time and the circumstances you face.

# CHAPTER 3

# Why Power Matters

You are as powerful as others perceive you to be. However, even if they regard you as being in a powerful position, this is no use to you unless you see the situation as they do.

> *"You only have power over people so long as you don't take everything away from them. When you've robbed a man of everything, he's no longer in your power – he's free again."*
>
> Aleksandr Solzhenitsyn

## WHAT DO WE MEAN BY POWER?

You are as powerful as others perceive you to be, which is limiting if you do not understand how they see the situation. Power can be real or perceived, or as subjective as it is objective in that it exists in people's heads; even though the other party may be dependent on you or independent of you. Power can shift, be created from timing and circumstance, can be used to nurture or exploit so clearly needs to be understood by the Complete Skilled Negotiator.

### *Why the balance of power matters*

So why is power so important in negotiations? Quite simply, it provides you with options and, if understood, will enable you to control where on the clock face your negotiation will take place.

- **Holding the balance of power.** If you hold the balance of power in your relationship(s), you have greater scope to control the agenda, the process and ultimately influence the negotiation in your favor.
- **Power to influence the climate, style, strategy and possibilities.** Meaning it provides you with the opportunity to choose between being competitive or collaborative depending on which suits your objectives.

Ultimately, providing a framework for determining objectively (rather than subjectively, which is so often the case) where the power sits between those involved. The ability to do this is critical if you are to perform as a Complete Skilled Negotiator.

#### Holding the balance of power

History has taught us that those with power will at some point seek to exercise it. Therefore it is vital to understand the balance of power, be clear where the negotiation is likely to take place on the clock face and prepare accordingly. The type of relationship you have with those you negotiate with will directly influence how and where you choose to negotiate on the clock face.

One of the most important considerations when gauging power will be the amount of *information* available relating to each party's circumstances. The degree to which circumstances are transparent directly affects the power balance within your relationship and the style of negotiation that is most likely to follow. That is not to suggest that those who enter a negotiation from a weak position enter as lambs ready for the slaughter: very often the more powerful party will use the situation to gain other forms of value such as loyalty, exclusivity or greater flexibility rather than just beating the other party into agreeing a low price. Where you negotiate on the clock face will impact on all these possibilities and the total value opportunity that will be created from your discussions. So we need to treat power respectfully if we are to make the most of it. The purpose of this is not so that you can win or beat the other party. They are not your competition. It is to help you realize as much value from the negotiations you are preparing for.

When the balance of power is clearly in favor of one party over the other, the negotiation is more likely to be based on **value distribution**. That is: "What you get, I lose and what I get, you lose." These win–lose negotiations are on the right-hand side of the clock face. Now you have the choice to let this happen, or to influence the clock face location by being proactive in your approach. Some people allow themselves to be victims of time and circumstances and blame power imbalance for the poor deals they secure. Others recognize the situation and take control, despite factors such as dependency which will serve to reduce their power.

**value distribution**
Where the value being negotiated is finite or fixed and the negotiation involves working out who will get how much from what is available as opposed to value creation where greater levels of value are created through low-cost/high-value trade-offs.

## Constraints on power in negotiation

Being proactive in your approach is nearly always worth the time and effort. However, it is also important to understand any imposed

**bidding process**
The bidding process which is defined and communicated by the auctioneer sets out the timing of bids, whether the duration is governed by time or number of bids, whether minimum bids or minimum increases are required and any other rules that allow the process to work between those involved.

constraints or parameters ahead of your negotiation. For instance, if you have ever entered a bidding war where the **bidding process** has been pre-defined by the organizers, and where your "competition" is unknown, you will know how it feels to be constrained and effectively disempowered. The bidding process has been designed to restrict all but your ability to counter-bid. Once the bidding has commenced you are effectively disempowered to do anything outside the process. The bidding process is there to ensure that the power is driven by competitive market pressures only. Any relationship issues become secondary as the auctioneer becomes as powerful as the interest and competition they have been able to introduce into the process. Trying to attract the best terms within a bidding process is like trying to negotiate with handcuffs on.

### *Power and understanding the individual*

Understanding your market, their options, the implications of change and so on may help you to gauge market power but, where you are involved in negotiating with any one person or company, you need to understand the personal circumstances and of course the nature of the person or people that you are dealing with. As we have learnt in history, in extreme cases of one-sided power, absolute power corrupts absolutely. The natural law of psychology provides those with power with such temptation that eventually they will use it to their own ends. The pressures and issues faced by an individual can be quite different from that suggested by the company they work for. Understanding this is critical, as understanding power in negotiation is just as important as is your competence to perform around the negotiation table. You must see through the company and understand the person. You negotiate with people, not companies.

### *Power and accountability*

Companies have brands, market share, capital, policies and hierarchy. However, business negotiations are conducted by representatives of companies, however large or small.

When negotiating, most people are accountable in some shape or form to others. They will be under some obligation to complete the deal on the "best possible terms," even if this means being flexible and creative to resolve differences. They will be working to time lines, have objectives to achieve, be accountable for their actions and be operating within a set of circumstances often not so dissimilar to those you face. They are engaged in the negotiation, which means there is some degree of motivation to do business. So, next time they tell you they have no interest in your proposal or in agreeing terms, ask yourself: "why are they still here then?" The essence of getting inside their head is about understanding their personal circumstances.

- What options do they have?
- What time pressures do they face?
- What premium would they place on a quick agreement?
- What issues for them carry the greatest value apart from price?

Remember, information is power.

## HOW DOES POWER INFLUENCE NEGOTIATIONS?

### *Influencing factors*

Those factors which have the greatest influence on where negotiations take place on the clock face are made up of the following:

1. The level of dependency.
2. The power of the brand and the relative size of both parties.
3. History/precedents.
4. Competitor activity and changing market conditions.
5. The party with more time.
6. The nature of the product, service or contract.
7. Personal relationships.

#### 1. The level of dependency

Who needs who the most, or the level of dependency between both parties, directly influences the balance of power between you and those you negotiate with. In economic terms it's referred to as supply and demand.

- If there is an abundance of supply and little demand, the buyers, assuming they have a need, will have more power available to them.
- If the product or service is in short supply yet demand is high, the seller will more likely have greater power.

In the commodity markets this basic economic principle is used to help determine prices on a whole range of products from diamonds to motor cars, oil, and even bananas – and ultimately that of the share prices of companies. Supply and demand, and sometimes scarcity, effectively set the parameters within which negotiations take place. They directly influence the options available to both parties and the level of dependency which exists.

Generally speaking, those with power will not only employ it but will usually find ways to exploit it. Creating power where you can control supply and demand can be a highly effective way of strengthening your negotiation position. For example, the oil industry has for many years controlled its output in terms of how many millions of barrels of oil are produced in any given week. This has a direct impact on the price of petrol at the pumps.

Where the balance of power is strongly in favor of one party and the need for cooperation during the negotiation is not necessary, that party can drive very tough negotiations. **Dependency imbalance** can result in the negotiation swinging around to the right-hand (competitive) side of the clock face.

**dependency imbalance**
This is where one party has a greater dependency on the other, resulting in them having no negotiating power.

In a business-to-business (B2B) context, absolute dependency leads to absolute power, which can promote corruption and make for poor business. This is why governments have competition and monopolies acts to manage extreme cases of non-competitive market manipulation. Creating options or a best alternative before entering your negotiation is an effective way of reducing dependency and, in doing so, reduce the power of the other party. Creating a **BATNA** (Best Alternative to a Negotiated Agreement) is therefore an important element of preparation (see Chapter 9). For as long as you have total dependency on one supplier or buyer, and assuming that they know this, you will be negotiating from a position of weakness.

**BATNA**
Best Alternative to a Negotiated Agreement.

## CASE STUDY

During the boom years of the 1990s Mercedes would spend millions of euros on the marketing of their latest C and E class ranges. Demand was high for these quality cars as motorists in the UK were being weaned off company car schemes through tax changes. This effectively gave motorists the opportunity to decide for themselves which car they wanted to drive. Mercedes were creative with their credit options, making these desirable vehicles affordable for those who, in the past, had been limited to a Ford or Vauxhall, depending on their own company car policy and agreement with lease companies. Mercedes controlled the volume of cars released into the UK and the allocation by dealership (supply and demand).

The waiting time for many vehicles was six months or more. Having already committed yourself psychologically to wanting the E class Mercedes, and convincing your partner that you could afford it with their creative, easy payment terms, you now had the prospect of negotiating for a vehicle that they could not even supply for six months. Demand was greater than supply. The dealerships were in a strong position not to negotiate over published prices. Meanwhile, a market grew in the UK based on the demand for high-quality cars. Bentley, Aston Martin, Ferrari and others, which sometimes had a two-year waiting list, attracted dealers who placed deposits on cars they did not want. With demand so high, they would go on to sell their "place" in the queue at a later date for a premium.

### Creating options

If you were going to buy a laptop and had decided to buy a Dell, this decision alone will have already narrowed your options in the market. Develop options and possibilities and then ensure the other party is aware that you have them. You may have based your decision on reliability, package price or any number of extras that Dell may offer. However, if you were prepared to accept a Toshiba, IBM, Samsung *or* a Dell, assuming you can get like-for-like features and add-ons, you will have increased your power and the likelihood of getting a better deal.

As the Complete Skilled Negotiator you should make the time to be proactive and plan out your options. Make the time to create alternatives and you will be able to manage the balance of power more effectively.

One challenge for account managers who manage only one customer is that the customer knows this and knows just how important they are to the account manager sat in front of them. Some accounts are so large that entire teams manage the one account and the buyer knows this too well. So who has the balance of power in this situation? As always it depends on the other six factors we are about to explore. For now I will suggest that the balance of power is not as one-sided as it may sometimes appear.

### 2. The power of the brand and the relative size of both parties

Imagine you are responsible for selling an established mega branded soft drink. You know that any retailer will sell more of your brand than their own brand or a lesser branded soft drink. The retailer accepts that margins will be lower due to the high investment in the brand itself, but this is offset by being able to sell higher quantities.

The retailer will probably sell their cheaper, higher-margin own brand as well, resulting in their overall product and margin mix being optimized.

Significant amounts of money are invested in building brands. As part of establishing the brands some manufacturers have even, for limited periods, supplied products to the distributors or retailers at no margin at all, or even at below cost. The aim here is to expose their product to the market as part of creating demand, brand awareness and attracting market share. In the long term, brand power and the terms which can be negotiated with a strong brand will more than outweigh the market entry costs.

In some cases, retail buyers need to stock certain lines in order to make their product category credible to their customers and also to remain competitive with other retailers. In doing so, they will list branded products despite having to operate at lower margins. So both extremes are in play here: brands are built and represent power within a negotiation in that the buyer needs them, but the same brands with which account managers need exposure to maintain their market share position can carry limited power. Who needs whom the most and why? What brands bring to the broader business case in terms of their reliability, quality and customer loyalty, will have some bearing on the considerations of the buyer, as they seek to optimize their profitability, starting by objectively weighing up the balance of power within the relationship.

### *Brand power*

Power, once created, will almost always be used in business. People or companies with power will use it to commercial advantage. I do not state this as being good or bad. It just is. Businesses invest in R&D, their brands and innovations to create a market position and therefore have earned or built the power they have. They may even have built their own power base in the market by narrowing down the competition, acquiring them, or their brands.

The investment in brand development provides the brand with "objective power," which helps those selling them to negotiate

**CASE STUDY**

A US jewelry chain, which held a major share of the global market, decided to negotiate longer payment terms with its suppliers. For the smaller suppliers of non-branded jewelry, a very demanding 4 o'clock hard bargaining negotiation occurred where the jewelry chain's power was exercised. However, when the chain negotiated with the major watch brands, the balance of power was much more balanced and as a result the negotiations took place on the more collaborative left-hand side of the clock face. In one case they were at 11 o'clock, discussing creative variables such as joint investment in overseas expansion opportunities and exclusive new lines.

The point to remember here is that, despite such brand power, you are still negotiating with people. Their pressures, hopes, objectives, options and priorities are often very different from those implied by the big brands that they represent and, to those negotiating, the pressures feel very real. Where the balance of power is more equal; negotiations are more likely to gravitate towards the left-hand, collaborative side of the clock face.

better terms. Brand credibility is built across all industry sectors, including banks, construction firms and car manufacturers, right down to local butchers. Businesses recognize how building brand differentiation and therefore loyalty can effectively provide power in their customers' decision-making process. Mega brands like Microsoft, Coca-Cola, Rolex, Apple, and dozens of others have benefited from creating negotiating power directly from brand power.

### 3. History/precedents

History and precedents also play a part in influencing how people seek to rationalize and legitimize their position: "Last time we agreed to a discount of 15% on volumes in excess of $3 million so let's start at 15%." Current terms can serve as the rationale for an **anchoring position** (see page 244, Chapter 8). Unless there is already a clear and agreeable rationale, many will demand that there is relativity between what has been agreed in the past and that which you are trying to agree for the future, unless you have the power to simply ignore previous dealings based on "that was then and this is now" or introduce such changes that any direct comparisons become distorted or invalid.

**anchoring position**
An opening position which serves to anchor the relative expectations and movement of the other party.

Previous positions, all else remaining equal, serve to shape expectations. Many organizations work hard to address this through the continuous innovation of products or changing the nature of the service they offer: they seek to remove the "apples for apples" comparisons. To achieve this, many may decide to:

- change the people responsible for the relationship;
- move historical understandings;
- change the package, service offer or product being supplied.

It is quite normal for organizations to do this as part of ensuring that trading remains competitive.

Historical agreements and precedents serve to provide us with anchors from which to negotiate. Often where change takes place, when a new person or team is assigned an account, or where a recent acquisition of a competitor takes place and new personalities come into play, objectives and motives of the "new players" can change quickly, bringing with them a move away from how the business will have been conducted in the past. Many organizations systematically move their buyers around so as to ensure that historical dealings can be ignored more easily.

In other cases, such as in corporate banking, great value is placed on established relationships and mutual experience which have taken years to build, and the value that these relationships offer can add to the collaborative way that the relationship is managed. In each case there is the knowledge of how business has been conducted in the past which is used to influence how it should be in the future.

#### 4. Competitor activity and market conditions

During the credit crunch in 2007/8, a period of unprecedented uncertainty was experienced by most industries in the US and across Europe. Commercial property prices, business values, future earnings forecasts, and ultimately earning multiples, were all severely hit. Companies with high levels of debt became more vulnerable and even companies with strong forward order books looked less secure. Market assumptions relating to risks were challenged; cash became king as commodity prices hit record highs along with the cost of oil and the radical shift in behavior of the banking industry. Literally within months, long-term commitments were difficult to attract as risk aversion became critical to survival. These changes had tested just about every forecast assumption, resulting in many contracts being negotiated or renegotiated in an entirely different climate and style to that of the original agreement.

The unpredictability of change affects the degree to which people are prepared to commit and the level of risk they are prepared to accommodate. In other words, stability and certainty promote a basis for longer-term commitments. In our ever-changing and fast-paced world, the issue of change plays an important part in any negotiation, in terms of what is being discussed, the length of any agreement and which party is more exposed to the influence of uncontrollable change.

Although change affects risk and value it can also affect power. Your competitors' innovation, marketing and strategy will have some bearing on what your customers regard as their options. The very fact that your competitors are competing provides more power to your customers during negotiations. For example, in electronics the launch of a new high-end, 60 inch, 3D, HD plasma TV that attracts 10% of the retail sales in its target market will directly affect sales of its competitors' TVs. This in turn will influence their trading performance and the power they have with their retail and wholesale customers.

**CASE STUDY**

A student living in Italy wanted to book a holiday to the US during the following year. Exchange rates and fuel prices were fluctuating, as were the prospects of greater Italian government green taxes being applied to long-haul flights. The tour operator had to somehow offer a price for a holiday based on certain assumptions. Under the terms of the booking, the tour operator was entitled to apply surcharges in the event of significant price changes. What if all three of these changes resulted in the student paying significantly more in surcharges to the point where they wouldn't be able to afford the holiday? What protection do they have and what level of risk are they carrying? To what degree has the tour operator factored in some of these risks to the pricing schedule, or insured themselves against them?

In a simple transaction such as booking a holiday, you can start to examine the risks associated with change that we cannot control and yet can still have an impact on the total cost of the deal on offer.

### 5. The party with more time

Time and circumstances offer the greatest of power levers in negotiation. If someone needs to sell immediately, for whatever reason, they are probably more likely to concede when under time pressure and circumstances are such that they have few options. If you have been effective at getting inside their head and understand their time pressures, you will have more power to exert. How you choose to use this will depend on your objectives, your relationship and the overall shape of the deal.

Time and circumstances are ever changing and because of this the value or perceived value of just about anything is constantly changing, which is why we should never assume the value or importance of any variable in the deal to the other party.

Your job as a negotiator is to test and qualify the priorities and interests of the other party all the time. Any company operating under pressure, whether it is to make a decision, place an offer, receive a delivery or conclude a deal, is compromised by time pressure and will already be placing a premium on doing whatever is necessary to meet their deadline. For you, understanding the pressures of the other party is the most obvious way of working out the balance of power within your relationship. However, a party who is prepared to pay more today as a result of time pressures may not be in the same position next week. So if you leave the opportunity too long you may lose the power you had as their circumstances improve.

In some cases, time and circumstances can be managed to create power for those who are proactive in sequencing their negotiations. For example, if you are about to negotiate with a number of customers or suppliers, the order of the sequencing of each negotiation, and the way the conclusions of those agreements are communicated to your remaining customers or suppliers, can influence the expectations, power and the behavior of those customers or suppliers who have yet to agree.

In David Lax and James Sebenius's book *3D Negotiation*, they describe how the third, often overlooked, dimension to negotiating is that of sequencing events through the mapping of processes, which helps create momentum and power. They describe how this differs from the way people traditionally interpret negotiations through

**CASE STUDY**

A team managing a buying group were keen to recruit a high performing buyer from a competitor and decided to make an approach. They had an informal meeting where the buyer explained that he was enjoying his current role and was not ready for a move, particularly because it would involve relocating. The director of the buying group accepted the buyer's position and they shook hands at the end of the meeting. As they did, the buyer handed the director a business card. Handwritten on the back of the card was the job title "Director of Buying" and a salary figure. "Call me when the time is good" said the buyer. Six months later he got the call. Indeed circumstances had changed, at which point the buyer made his career move.

tactics and behavior only. Sequencing allows you to manage dependency on time and circumstances to provide a set of circumstances which allow you to control power through the circumstances faced by those involved.

### 6. The nature of the product, service or contract

Negotiating a complex construction deal or business merger is, by its very nature, more challenging than buying a car from your local garage. Alternatively, agreeing a contract for IT services, by its very nature, requires a different type of process and agenda than, say, agreeing a settlement following a marriage breakdown. The different relationships in play and the nature of the outcomes required result in most negotiations being unique.

*Example: buying a car*

If you were buying a second-hand car privately, you would probably set about agreeing a price with the current owner. Two pieces of information would help set the parameters for discussion. Firstly the price that the owner is asking, which is effectively their opening position, and secondly, what the model and age of car would typically sell for in the market. Both parties will be aware of this and usually end up negotiating around the price. The buyer may seek to lower the seller's aspirations by pointing to some work that the car needs doing to bring it up to scratch. The seller may try to increase its perceived value by promoting the reliability of the car and the fact that it has only had one owner. Neither argument need make any difference to the negotiation unless you choose to listen to them. There is no prospect of a relationship following the deal, few issues to negotiate around, so a Hard Bargaining or Deal Making negotiation is likely to follow (4–5 o'clock on the clock face).

Now imagine you were in a position to spend more money and decided to purchase from a local dealer. Can the worn tire be replaced? Will they tax the car? Can they provide competitive finance arrangements? Both the possibility of a relationship beyond the immediate agreement and a broader agenda to discuss could result in the negotiation being more appropriately conducted in a Concession Trading or even a Win–Win environment (7–8 o'clock on the clock face).

Finally, consider the same transaction, but this time you are considering buying a new car from a main dealer. Servicing, depreciation and future trade-in guarantees, extras on the car and even insurance now start to feature in your discussions. Total value becomes a greater consideration and the deal may well take place in a Joint Problem Solving or even a Relationship Building environment (10–11 o'clock on the clock face).

What has changed over these three scenarios is the breadth of issues which can be discussed and the possibility of a relationship which goes beyond that of the transaction. The item, a car, remains broadly the same but in each case the appropriate style of negotiation changes.

*Example: outsourcing a cleaning contract*

Imagine you were in the process of agreeing to outsource a cleaning contract. Issues such as standards, quality, reliability, performance reviews and contract length would also feature. With up to twenty issues to discuss and a relationship to follow you may conclude that a win–win negotiation at 8 o'clock may be the appropriate style to adopt.

However, if the balance of power is strongly in your favor (for example, you might have ten companies keen to work with you who are all in a position to meet your requirements at a similar price point), you may choose to dictate the terms to your chosen supplier, negotiating a Hard Bargaining deal at 4 o'clock, or even put the opportunity out to tender at 2 o'clock. Again this may help you secure a good short-term deal, but then you may carry the risk that the "winners" of the contract prove unable or unwilling to fulfil the performance requirements of the agreement. In this case, the prospect of the inconvenience of changing suppliers and the time taken performance managing and terminating the agreement should motivate you to think of more balanced ways of managing the negotiation, as a means of leaving them motivated to deliver a quality service level.

*There is no right or wrong.* Your responsibility as a negotiator is to weigh up what you are trying to achieve and decide which process is more likely to cover the broad range of risks and benefits involved.

### 7. Personal relationships

In every culture, relationships and trust play a part in the climate of negotiations. Building an understanding of each other's position and needs through exploratory meetings is critical if broader agendas other than price are to be entertained. For instance, areas covering joint risks and other value-adding possibilities, such as specification, joint investment and managing risk, could be explored. Most people prefer doing business with people they trust and respect. The degree to which trust exists will almost always influence the climate of openness and the position on the clock face where the negotiation takes place.

However, we must not confuse trust and respect with being liked. Many people have an inherent need to be liked which, if they are not careful, can result in unnecessary and unconditional concessions that can erode value in the short term on the assumption that they will reciprocate at some point in the future. It's possible to operate in this way but only where the relationship is strong enough and only where the consequences of a relationship breakdown are detrimental to your long-term interests.

Respect has to be earned and is more likely to be achieved through being tough, consistent and reliable rather than by being over-flexible or agreeing to make unconditional concessions. Even if you feel others are being unfair, inconsiderate, unyielding or even arrogant in their dealings, your role is to look beyond behavior and make a rational, sober, unemotional assessment of the balance of power. Emotional responses to the positions and demands of the other party will only play to their advantage. Similarly, if you are in a position of strength, use it to assert your position and gain commitments, but not to aggravate the situation. Remember that negotiation is not about "winning" in the sense of beating the other party.

Being generous leads to greed rather than appreciation: concessions which on reflection could be considered unnecessary are sometimes excused in order to "keep the relationship on track." Some people deceive themselves into thinking that it is necessary and justify it by saying that without certain concessions, cooperation would have been difficult to maintain. Yet, in all my experience as a negotiator, I have found that generosity promotes greed. The more you give, the more the other party will want. It does little to promote the necessary mutual respect that is essential to promote business relationships.

It is true that without some degree of trust your negotiations are likely at best to feel transactional and difficult. Equally, with too much familiarity, complacency kicks in and the total value, and the value opportunity, becomes compromised. It is for this reason that many companies systematically change their buyers around to ensure that relationships do not stand in the way of good business. The challenge for you is to find the right balance between formality and understanding.

## CIRCUMSTANCES WHICH INFLUENCE POWER

Power registers only when it is credible, believable and exercisable. However, there are many lessons from history that support the notion that the perception of power can work equally as well as real power derived by facts known to both parties.

Creating the perception of power *before* the negotiation begins can be achieved through demonstrating indifference, outlining the other party's options or the current terms they are operating on, all of which are designed to manage expectations and suggest that they are negotiating from a position of strength. Trying to do so once discussions have begun is transparent and can prove futile. Negotiators have used their skills in positioning over the years to achieve this. The Complete Skilled Negotiator understands the value of clearly framing the facts surrounding the circumstances of those involved so as to improve their perceived power.

The primary factors which influence the power between you and the other party are:

- need and dependency;
- time and circumstance;
- threats and consequences;
- supply and demand (scarcity); and
- information, transparency and knowledge.

The balance of power can be as much about your perception of power as it is about any real objective measure. Central to any power balance in negotiation is how need and dependency are viewed. Who needs whom the most, or at all? The fact that both parties are sitting at the table talking indicates that there is some interest in conducting business, yet power, or the perception of power, will play a significant part in how the negotiation progresses. First you must understand power, then build it and finally decide on how you will deploy it.

### *Need and dependency*

Need and dependency are at the core of the balance of power. If you don't need to do a deal and are not dependent on the other party your position of "indifference" provides you with a high level of power, assuming that you both know this and believe it to be true – the main reason why negotiators work so hard at remaining indifferent during meetings. Any need to form an agreement is usually influenced by your circumstances, whatever they may be. What need and dependency mean to you will be unique to each relationship and each situation.

The professional poker player recognizes that his hand is as strong as the hand he believes the other players to have. It is this understanding that the players calculate before deciding on which type of game to play. In their own head they may become vulnerable as they consider the strength of their own hand, so they switch their attention to the habits and body language of the other players to work out the strength of the other hands before making their move.

It is important to understand power and how it impacts on your expectations and those of the other party. The way most people gauge power is from instinctive subjective insights formed from observations of the other party or more often on clear factual market evidence. If you are the only supplier who can deliver what your customer cannot do without, they are likely to pay as much as they need to get what they want. Of course few relationships are so one-sided or remain so for very long. Power is often measured in a subjective manner, meaning that feelings, instinct, circumstance and behavior also contribute to the way you weigh up any given situation.

**CASE STUDY**

Carlos Silva ran a franchise car hire operation at a regional Spanish airport. One evening, the last flight into the airport was delayed and, when it finally arrived, other car hire firms had closed for the night. It was a Friday and Carlos had had a poor week in sales. He needed one more car hire to make his target for the week, which is why he decided to stay open in the knowledge that there was still one delayed flight due to arrive. A businessman came to his desk and said that he needed to hire a car there and then. The businessman, looking distressed, said that this was the only car hire desk left open. Carlos knew this already. He also knew that there were no other supply routes available to the businessman (supply and demand). The businessman had a need, and time and circumstances were against him. This left Carlos in a very strong position. Had he been in his own head he might have just taken the order, relieved that he had now achieved his target for the week. However, Carlos decided to ask questions to find out the businessman's position, check out his circumstances, qualify his options, define his absolute dependency and then he hired out the biggest car he had available in the fleet for twice the cost of a car from his budget range. He used his power. He offered limited information about the options he had available and maximized the opportunity. The businessman was so relieved to get a car, that size and price had become secondary issues.

**CASE STUDY**

A local convenience grocery store had a policy of buying and selling local produce wherever possible. Their customers liked it and the local farmers benefited from this policy. There were two local farms that produced pork, from which bacon, sausages, pork chops, trotters and even pigs' ears were purchased. One of the farmers decided to retire and sell his small farm. The purchaser of the farm was a local dairy farmer who decided not to continue with the pig farming and that the supply of pork from this farm would cease. This left the convenience retailer with only one source of pork from the remaining local pig farmer. Over the coming months, the remaining pig farmer increased his prices. The retailer continued to order reasonable volumes due to his commitment to source locally. The retail grocer, who operated twenty stores, recognized the power he had clearly lost due to the lack of local competition and his commitment to source locally. He decided to approach the dairy farmer with a proposition. He proposed a joint venture which guaranteed orders of 50% of his total pork requirements for a three-year period, offering to pay the same high prices that he was already paying to the only other pig farmer. The margin opportunity convinced the dairy farmer to invest in pork. Within three months of trading, the retailer was able to renegotiate with the original pig farmer to bring his rates back down to a level below where they had been a year earlier. He used the threat of moving all of his business across to the ex-dairy farmer with whom he had created a "joint investment" as a means of ensuring highly competitive pricing.

On the many occasions I have facilitated negotiation planning sessions across teams with various clients, I ask the question about power: "Who has the balance of power in your business relationship, you or the buyer/seller?'" On over 70% of occasions, the initial response is: "the other party!" Why? Because most of us live in our own head. We find it difficult to see, feel, or understand the pressures that the other party is experiencing, so we focus on those to which we are exposed and this of course undermines our own position of power. Negotiating from inside your own head is a very dangerous place to be. The balance of power between those involved in the majority of negotiations is much closer than most will allow themselves to believe.

As a Complete Skilled Negotiator it is important to recognize that even where the market power is clearly stacked against you, you can set out to change the dependencies between you and the other party over time as part of shifting the balance of power.

### *Time and circumstance*

Many business leaders have remarked that their successful negotiations are commonly due to good timing. Get the timing right and the tables are in your favor. But what if the timing of a deal is not naturally in your favor? The other party could have many options and can reject your ideas and proposals. The answer is to orchestrate events in such a way that you build power by taking control of time and circumstance. But how can this be possible?

If time and circumstances affect options, then, by creating circumstances through the sequencing of events, you can effectively

## CASE STUDY

A tire distribution company based in Brazil had an agreement to supply a number of retailers and tire and exhaust specialists. In Brazil you can buy tires alongside your groceries. Recently under new ownership, the tire distributor was entering their annual price increase negotiations and planned to introduce an average 8% increase across their customer base. Each customer was categorized by size and channel. The tire company further analyzed where conditions existed which would allow them to secure both early wins (agreements) and were more likely to attract a commitment without serious implications. These smaller customers were positioned in phase one of discussions which took four weeks to complete. As negotiations were concluded, the agreements were announced to the press. At the time, phase two was commencing with some of the more challenging negotiations. Some precedents were in place (early agreements from phase one) which implied that the prices were being accepted in the market and passed through to consumers. The toughest category of customers was saved till phase three, but made up only 30% market share from their final thee customers. Since 70% had already been agreed, this provided greater power to the tire distribution business. They were now in a credible position and could if necessary threaten to invest more with their phase one and two customers, if the phase three customers were not prepared to agree. The phasing of the negotiations had created power and momentum which made agreements across all customers possible.

build power in your favor. In other words, you can take control, of the time and circumstances enabling you to negotiate from a greater position of power. This can include the development of options (your BATNAs – Best Alternative To a Negotiated Agreement), the order in which you hold discussions to further qualify your BATNAs, and the order you agree, especially when you need to agree terms with a number of customers or suppliers.

This type of approach is used across many industries by those who are strategic in their approach and proactive in their planning. In the case of the tire company, had a unilateral demand been sent to all customers and responses managed in a reactive manner, the outcome would have been far less certain.

### *Threats and consequences*

Where threats and consequences are put before you it is important to qualify their validity. Does the other party have the power to carry the threats out? Are they bluffing or is it for real? If they do will it harm them? Do they really have the options they say they have?

Although transparency helps to wipe away some of the "mist" when deciding the difference between real and implied threats, you need to gain as much clarity as possible. Without this clarity, you will be operating from an unclear if not compromised position, regardless of what the balance of power within your relationship might suggest.

One difference when negotiating with your family is that most threats are transparent and you will understand whether they have the power to exercise them. Within your own business and across your business it is easier to qualify the likelihood of a threat being carried out. However, with customers and suppliers, especially in new relationships, it can be far more challenging to distinguish between the signals provided and the reality.

### Tactical play

Tactics can be used as a way of delivering implied threats or consequences used to manipulate a situation. This is sometimes done through introducing false time lines or ultimatums which have been introduced by a higher authority such as the other party's boss. These are used when trying to apply pressure or to create urgency. If the other party attempts to apply these, qualify them. Ask them what will happen and explore what would happen next without asking the types of leading questions which result in you digging a hole for yourself such as "so you have no movement on this issue then?" The idea behind qualifying such claims is to try and establish if they really will or can exercise them or if gamesmanship is in play. Of course they are never going to admit to this so it is your role to gauge the likelihood of risk, given all the information you can gather.

It is also prudent to note that threats are not always hollow and may indeed be carried out. In the film *The Godfather*, Vito Corleone was renowned for his proposal: "I'm gonna make him an offer he can't refuse." For most, their own life was too high a price for any concession, and believing that the Don would carry out the threat, and that the Corleone family was a greater force than they could overcome, the recipient would concede. Those calling his bluff would face the consequences.

In business, threats, although rarely so extreme, can still be devastating and may deliver consequences such as loss of business, loss of reputation and so on. However, if you hold power over another by virtue of a threat that you can exercise, the power only exists until the threat is exercised. Once the victim has been freed from the fear of consequence they themselves may become dangerous in their behavior. Nothing is quite as sweet as revenge and we all have long memories.

### CASE STUDY

A branded cereals manufacturer was placed in an awkward position by one of the largest grocery retailers which was demanding more financial investment to help them compete. The retailer outlined the consequences of not helping them, in that they would at first start to reduce the range of products they stocked from the manufacturer, followed by not stocking any new innovative products until an agreement was in place. A time line was set whereby the ultimate threat, a total de-listing of all products, would be exercised. The manufacturer, at first extremely concerned by the prospect, conducted an analysis of the situation. Without disclosing their predicament, they conversed with other leading grocers offering to increase their investment with them in return for significant growth opportunities. They effectively worked on a BATNA that helped rebalance power during the negotiations which followed with the retailer. They then adopted an assertive strategy in response to the de-listing by withholding stock on all other lines. They were prepared to exit the relationship (for now) if it was necessary. The negotiation was quickly escalated up through the ranks of the retailer, and within a month the retailer conceded, accepting a new set of terms similar to those the supplier was originally operating on.

### *Supply and demand*

If power is directly affected by circumstance then supply and demand represents one of the main issues that influence it. Quite simply, if there is a shortage or difficulty in acquiring something, assuming that demand is stable or strong, then the value will increase. In times of no demand or when there is oversupply the value or price will generally drop. Although this is the case in most market situations it is not always so apparent. Asking the right questions will help you to clarify this:

- How is your supplier performing generally, and how important does this make you to them?
- How many options other than you do they have to achieve their strategic objectives?
- If demand for the product has slowed, how much more important has this made your agreement?

Buying and selling commodities provides the clearest illustration of how the market (those wanting to buy and those wanting to sell) effectively sets its own price. The price of petrol at the pumps, the price of coffee, sugar, gold and even bananas is influenced by the supply in the market and demand. The price of steel in recent years has grown dramatically as demand from China has left other economies effectively competing for supply and as a result the market prices have risen. The simple economic truth is that supply and demand set the parameters within which we trade and within which we are able to negotiate.

Why does one company buy out its competitor? To build its market share? Perhaps. To create synergies in its cost base and operating costs? Perhaps. To remove a competitor, allowing it to trade more freely with greater power in its market? Almost definitely. When we hear of company mergers that have fallen short of the benefits outlined for the merger in the first place, it is the obvious short-term, cost-base saving which is cited. However, over the longer term, the market position and power to trade more effectively are often understated.

### CASE STUDY

During December 2009, the UK had an unusually high level of snow. Our local garden centre had back stocks of over 250 plastic sledges from the previous year when there had been no snow fall. Children had just finished school for the Christmas break, their parents were finishing their work commitments and every hill in the area was covered with families making the most of the snow. A sign was promptly erected at the garden centre entrance: "Sledges for sale £9.99." The garden centre sold half of their sledges in two days. By now the snow was starting to melt. As demand for the sledges dropped, the price was changed on the sign to £6.99. On the third day, the manager dropped the price to £4.99, after taking the view that the snow was melting and that most of the locals would already have bought a sledge by now. On the fourth day (the 23 December), there was another unexpected snow fall. The manager changed the price back to £9.99 and sold out of sledges by Christmas Eve. The price, as in any market situation, was set to reflect demand rather than simply the cost price of the item plus a margin.

So, with demand you have options in that if one party is not interested another will be. The more demand you are able to create, the more options you have, and the more powerful your position will be in just about any type of negotiation.

Although not always possible, one of the most effective ways of building power for yourself is by developing BATNAs, because the more options you have, the stronger you become.

The clearer your options, the more definitive your own breakpoint will be.

Understanding and building options or BATNAs is fundamental to establishing power. **No options = no power**, or at least from inside your own head.

The supply of money on the money markets influences the best mortgage rates available for home buying. These rates are regularly published in the press as banks compete to lend money against the security of property. Some take the time to talk to a mortgage broker who will provide a range of options based on their circumstances; some will approach the bank or mortgage company who will outline their latest offer, or they may simply be advised of the cost of extending their current mortgage without providing any other options. However, those who genuinely shop around, research the internet and talk with a number of suppliers effectively get a feel for what the best on the market is. Along with a BATNA, knowing what you can get elsewhere ensures that the time invested in research pays off. The best deals are not necessarily the ones advertised. In the world of private banking there are many deals available for the right person at below high street prices subject to the right relationship and broader circumstances. With a high street BATNA to hand it's worth progressing such discussions.

Qualifying the other party's options, and therefore their power, requires us to question objectively the viability of the options they say they have. In some industries there are substantial costs in implementing an option. For instance, the set-up costs of switching manufacturers may be considerable: re-tooling, resourcing materials, new safety inspections; not to mention the disruption and ongoing training and relationship-building that needs to take place. The other party may be able to employ their BATNA, but they may be unwilling to actually implement it.

If you could read the minds of the other party you would be able to see the options available, understand their true cost base, their time pressures, and the real implications of having no agreement, and so on. Unfortunately, such transparency rarely exists. However, you can still unearth some of this information by questioning, exploring and listening to various stakeholders to understand the circumstances of the other party.

Imagine the early prospectors in the Gold Rush. They sat by the river, panning through tons of silt to find the "nuggets" that would one day make them rich. In this information age you should regard information nuggets as being equally as valuable. Building a picture and getting into the other party's head requires research, analysis, exploratory meetings, studying past precedents, their current strategy and questioning to test assumptions. Most large organizations have resources to help: market research, consumer insight and knowledge management departments, all of which can add tremendous value to the understanding of their customers. This value more than offsets the cost of these departments and those who work in them.

Information about the other person's options or circumstances certainly provides power and for the same reasons you should seriously consider how much information and what type of information is appropriate for you to share with them. Building power requires you to think and operate like a barrister, but not an interrogator, questioning appropriately to glean those "information nuggets", or insights as to where the nuggets are. Approach the issues from different angles. This is not about interrogating as we have to manage the relationships involved. It is about understanding the whole situation; using your curiosity, inquisitiveness and desire to clarify the issues as they see them. The more you invest in understanding their motives, objectives and, often, their bottom line, the more powerful your position becomes and for this you need to exercise patience.

### *Information, transparency and knowledge*

Power can be derived from information. Your motive for gaining information about the other person is so that you can ascertain where they believe the balance of power is, based on their circumstances.

Time and circumstances, supply and demand and even the other party being totally reliant on you can only provide you with power if you understand what these factors mean from inside their head. If you do not, they will offer you no power and as a result no advantage. It is for this reason that questioning and listening are critical behaviors of negotiators. Negotiating in a vacuum (not

## CASE STUDY

Following two years of applications and meetings, a supplier of training services specializing in Change Management secured a one-year contract, part of which was to be recognized as the preferred training provider to the Australian government. Their services would be readily available across a number of government departments for managers to attend courses as part of a range of planned management change programmes. The owners of the training company were delighted to secure the 12-month contract: they knew that they had both a very powerful offer and one that was tailored specifically to meet the needs of civil servants. Terms were keenly negotiated and the training courses began. The contract was going well and after nine months the supplier was invited to re-tender for the contract. Within weeks a negotiation began with the Australian government's central procurement function representing each of the government departments. What the training firm had not understood was that they were the only specialist supplier who had both met the requirements set out by the government and the only supplier of these services who had ever managed to consistently deliver to the specifications outlined in the original contract document. They were the only credible supplier in the market who could deliver the service and the government team knew it. However, the training supplier, fully aware of who they thought their competition was, were unaware of this fact. So keen were they to hold on to their contract they reduced their prices by 20% in a desperate attempt to secure a new three-year agreement. Had they been able to secure more information about their competitors' behavior, let alone their customers' view of their competitors, their own view of the balance of power may well have resulted in a different outcome. They remained in their own head throughout discussions. The power of information would have dramatically affected the outcome of the agreement. This information only came to light years later when they hired an ex-employee from the same procurement department they had negotiated with.

understanding the market around you) can only result in you operating inside your own head and therefore suboptimizing your opportunities.

Quite simply, information is power.

## CREATING POWER THAT PROVIDES CONTROL

### *Parallels between physics and psychology*

Of course even if you believe you have power it is only of any use if employed. It's no good having a power plant ready and capable of supplying millions of watts of electricity if no one can be bothered to turn on a light switch. Using power to create motion or movement is best understood when we consider the definitions provided by Newton's three Laws of Motion which translate well to the psychological realities of negotiation. Newton's laws have been studied for over 200 years in the physical context but when applied to business relationships provide highly relevant similarities to those circumstances found in negotiations and are those which are understood and deployed by the Complete Skilled Negotiator.

1. Newton's Law of Inertia – Proactivity

This law suggests that: "*an object at rest or in uniform motion in a straight line will remain at rest or in the same uniform motion unless acted upon by an unbalanced force.*"

This is also known as the "law of inertia."

This is often the position taken up by those with power in negotiations. In negotiations you need to employ proactivity to create momentum and in turn negotiating power. By exercising a force, you can promote movement or a response by the other party, which is effectively designed to overcome their inertia. In other words, if you do nothing, expect nothing to change. It is your actions that will bring about change through the use of what power you have available to you or what power you are able to create.

These activities can take the form of introducing:

- new time constraints;
- new alternatives;
- a new proposal; or
- a threat to terminate.

If the other party's inertia comes from them believing that they don't have to make a move or be flexible, your proactive use of

**CASE STUDY**

An Italian furniture manufacturer specializing in reproduction wooden furniture sourced its raw materials from five different wholesale suppliers. Two of these wholesalers specialized in oak and had supplied the manufacturer for the past 15 years. One of the suppliers, a large national supplier, decided to impose a 7% annual price increase using a general shortage of the supply of French, American and British oak for its reasoning. They were adamant that they would not move on their new pricing, which would come into effect immediately. The second of the two oak suppliers had also written to the furniture manufacturer, advising them of their annual price review of 2.5% which had been consistent over the past five years. The manufacturer challenged the 7% increase with the first supplier and counter-proposed with 2.5% to be in line with the market. The first supplier explained that other suppliers were likely to have more back stock to work through, but that it would only be a matter of time before they too would be forced to increase prices. The manufacturer remained intransigent and would not move from their 2.5% offer. However, they were no strangers to the market and didn't find the prospect of sourcing oak through just one supplier appealing as they believed it would make them vulnerable in the long term. As a short-term measure, they introduced other suppliers, even at short-term rates that were not as keen as those that had been achieved from their first supplier who was threatening to increase prices by 7%. Their actions caused the first supplier to back down and eventually concede (within two weeks) to a 2.5% increase. However, this was also negotiated on the basis of other terms. The furniture manufacturer finally agreed to improve the first supplier's longevity of its own cost base by agreeing to longer-term agreements, three-month notice periods for any future terms changes, and a strategy outlining their plans to ensure sustainable sources at competitive prices.

positioning and implied consequence (derived from power) can help you to challenge their assumption.

To create movement, you could insist on agreeing on a process for developing an agenda:

- Ask them what else is important to them?
- What are the risks they envisage?
- What or who else needs to be involved?

**negotiating agenda**
A list of variables which make up the scope and provide the parameters for the pending negotiation.

Your proactivity will ensure in the first instance that there is ongoing dialogue; in the second, that you have an expectation that other issues will be negotiated. The fixed price list, the historical terms or the high-end brand, all of which suggest that they are non-negotiable, are there to be challenged. In these situations you can make use of the **negotiating agenda** to focus the attention of the other party on the broader implications of the deal and signal that, even if the price has to remain fixed, other terms are there to be negotiated.

If nothing is agreed until everything is agreed then the agenda is there to help ensure that all areas have been covered before the final deal is struck. Equally, once the agenda is agreed you can, if desired, legitimately reject issues introduced later during discussions on the basis that "they were never part of this deal," and that your proposals to date had not taken those particular issues into account. In other words, an agreed agenda allows you to have some control over the parameters of the deal.

So negotiations often take place over what is on or off the agenda before the negotiation in earnest even gets started. This is often seen in trade union negotiations. Taking control of agreeing the agenda items also allows you:

- to set out the points which should be included in discussions and the points which should remain out of scope; and
- to narrow or broaden the scope of discussions and even imply timescales for discussions.

Fees, margin or price will always be important points, but the broader agenda must reflect the issues that are likely to either cost you or provide more security or value from the deal.

Also, by outlining the issues and inviting the other party to contribute to or change the agenda, you are promoting joint ownership by involving them, and gaining buy-in and acceptance that both parties' issues will need to be agreed as part of the deal. By managing this communication in advance of the meeting you are more likely to be able to position and prioritize the agenda issues to suit your needs.

Ultimately the party who is proactive with scoping and communication is more likely to be the one controlling the events and, in doing so, influencing their position of power and reducing the risk of inertia when negotiating.

### 2. Newton's Law of Acceleration

This law suggests that: "*an object moves in the direction that you push it. If you push it twice as hard, it will accelerate twice as fast, but the greater the mass, the slower the acceleration.*"

This is also known as "the law of acceleration."

Changes in movement through a time frame depend on the other party: often a function of size and force applied to it as energy (power) is transferred. The faster you drive at an opponent in rugby or American football, the more force you are able to exert. The bigger you are (the more weight), the more force you have to exert. In negotiation, the more able you are at creating momentum, even if you are not as big or powerful as you believe the other party to be, the more likely they are to respond to your presence.

Newton's law suggests that any physical item travelling at speed will have an impact weight many times its dormant weight. In negotiation, the power you have within your relationship can be increased through sequencing and controlling the process through time, options and circumstances.

**CASE STUDY**

A bank decided to introduce a unilateral price increase to all its business customers, notifying them by letter of the changes in terms and that the change was immediate. It was positioned as a given, where the letter simply confirmed the changes and implied that all customers were now operating on the new terms. Although the bank was only dealing with 30 sizable businesses, each of whom were important to its business, the positioning and timing of the letter ensured that over 90% of clients agreed without further negotiation. The directors of the bank later agreed that, had they visited each client for meetings to discuss the changes prior to the announcement, a much lower success rate would have been achieved.

3. Newton's Third Law of Motion – Reaction

This law suggests that: "*For every action, there is an equal and opposite reaction.*"

This is also known as "the law of reaction."

If one object exerts a force on a second object, the second object exerts a force equal in magnitude and opposite in direction. If you kick a ball by swinging your leg first and then exerting force through your muscle, the power of the motion which hits the ball through your foot transfers to the ball. The ball is then travelling at a speed consistent with the power used to strike it. In negotiation, if you force the issue, they may capitulate like the ball when kicked. However, if the other party is powerful (represented by a ball made of iron) you may find yourself with a bruised foot. So before you exert power, qualify the response you expect and carry out a reality check on whether the reaction will prove to be too painful.

## CONCLUSION

In Chapter 2 we looked at the three factors that influence every negotiation:

1. Power.
2. Trust.
3. Understanding total value and mutual opportunities.

In Chapter 3, we have explored in detail the dynamics of power in negotiations (such as time and circumstances), and how trust (relationships) can also be linked to the balance of power. The next chapters look at how certain behaviors and traits can affect outcomes of negotiations and how the use of these will help you perform as a Complete Skilled Negotiator.

# CHAPTER 4

# The Ten Negotiation Traits

Self-awareness comes from knowing and being honest with yourself about who you are, what you do and how you perform.

Most people like to regard themselves as good negotiators. Yet when asked why they think they perform well, they can usually only describe a few of their strengths, or things they believe make a difference to their performance. If the clock face has taught us anything, it has demonstrated that different types of negotiation require different skills. In other words, Hard Bargaining at 4 o'clock on the clock face requires strengths that are different from those required to perform effectively when Joint Problem Solving at 10 o'clock. However, before moving on to examine how to adapt your behavior as you move around the clock face it is worth understanding how personal traits can influence your overall ability when trying to secure the best deal. To a sports professional, examples of relevant traits might be stamina, agility, speed and flexibility. These will be important to different degrees, depending on the sport they specialize in. They help to define a player's potential and those which require further development as part of improving their overall performance. Some traits are innate and some can be learned or improved on. Importantly these traits underpin the player's ability to behave and perform to the highest levels in competitive environments.

Providing corporations with a standard to negotiate with has been made easier with the holistic approach symbolized by the Complete Skilled Negotiator. Understanding power is important if you are to exercise your commercial acumen and utilize the clock face. Developing behaviors (Chapter 5) will help you perform and optimize opportunity. Understanding yourself, and the personal traits which best serve you in negotiation, offers a further dimension and one that through greater self-awareness will allow you to play to your strengths.

The ten negotiation traits I have outlined directly influence the actions you take and they can be developed through a more conscious approach to how you negotiate. They relate to those attributes which come more naturally to you or those you are more likely to gravitate towards. What is important here is that you think about how these traits influence you and your performance when you negotiate. The ten traits underpin your behavior. For example, maintaining your nerve supports your ability to think clearly when faced with conflict and to open a negotiation with an extreme and yet realistic position. If you handle pressure well, and have the nerve to maintain self-control comfortably, your performance in tougher negotiations where competitive behaviors are required will come more naturally. Your traits are neither good nor bad; they are just a reflection of who you are. The important point is to understand yourself well enough to compensate for that which does *not* come naturally and of course to use your strengths to your advantage.

| The Ten Traits |
| --- |
| 1. Nerve |
| 2. Self-discipline |
| 3. Tenacity |
| 4. Assertiveness |
| 5. Instinct |
| 6. Caution |
| 7. Curiosity |
| 8. Numerical reasoning |
| 9. Creativity |
| 10. Humility |

## 1. NERVE:

### Believe in your position, never offend and always remain calm

Nerve helps us to exercise patience and to remain calm when the pressure is on. Anyone operating under pressure is reliant on controlling their nerves as part of being able to perform. The pilot, golfer, police officer, barrister, to name but a few, rely on their nerve to be able to carry out their duties as does the negotiator.

Exercising nerve during negotiations involves handling both perceived and real conflict, being able to read the sensitivities around the situation and calculate the risks before responding. Nothing happens by accident in negotiation, so having a clear head that allows you to operate as a **conscious negotiator** is essential to staying in control. Nerve also allows you to introduce challenging opening positions where appropriate in the knowledge in that you are taking a risk that could compromise the potential of a deal. It allows you to more easily demonstrate conviction when taking up a position with confidence.

**conscious negotiator**
A conscious negotiator is aware of their surroundings and the effect that they have on the relationship and the deal. Every action is intentional and considered. There is a high state of awareness and intent. They recognize that negotiation is uncomfortable and the job in hand requires them to accommodate this rather than allowing themselves to relax and become vulnerable.

Opening with an extreme position and remaining silent where appropriate might be described in some contexts as aggressive or even arrogant. Yet when combined with humility, and when remaining calm, exercising nerve can make for a very effective, if not tough negotiation stance. Without nerve you are more likely to become a victim of your discomfort, lose respect and ultimately concede more readily. With nerve comes the ability to move position when you are ready and only when it is appropriate.

### 2. SELF-DISCIPLINE:

**To understand what to do, and to do that which is appropriate**

Self-discipline: it's an everyday term, yet in negotiation it requires you to separate your behavior from your feelings and emotions.

It allows you to be what you need to be and what the situation demands of you, rather than behaving in a way that satisfies your own emotions. Self-discipline does not require you to be a different person, but to fulfil the role requirements at the time to help you perform. For example, remaining indifferent about the potential of a proposal which has been made may be more appropriate than showing any overt enthusiasm or excitement. Having the self-discipline to resist showing emotion helps you remain calm in appearance. This is not to suggest that you should remain indifferent to all proposals made in your negotiations, but to be disciplined enough that you present the signals you want the other party to read.

Actors understand how to behave deliberately when delivering a line, both verbally and non-verbally. They orchestrate the behavior of their characters as a conscious competent performer, and are able to retain their composure. The difference is that they are working with a script, whereas for the Complete Skilled Negotiator there is no script.

Patience and the ability to handle frustration is a quality found in most experienced negotiators. It is highly frustrating trying to get the other party to agree to something they appear reluctant to do. However, this can be achieved by the use of:

- good timing;
- summarizing;
- repackaging the offer;
- remaining at ease with silence; and
- having the self-control to avoid selling your position or talking inappropriately.

Having achieved this within yourself you need, of course, to ensure that where you are negotiating in a team, the remainder of the team are equally as well disciplined.

### 3. TENACITY:

#### The negotiator's equivalent to stamina

The times you hear the dreaded words "no, can't, won't" are the occasions where you will have to turn to "how." Rather than simply concede on the issue, you should seek to examine the rejection from different perspectives to find out what other conditions or circumstances you could introduce as part of maintaining control and managing their expectations. For instance, in tennis if your opponent breaks your serve, you don't give up on the set, you work harder in the next game to regain your position.

**the "broken record" tactic**
Repeating yourself is a way to assert a position without backing down or losing control. This also works well in negotiation as a counter tactic, when the other party is seeking to wear your position down.

There will be times when it is appropriate to hold firm and test the other negotiator's resolve. If you can truly operate inside the other party's head then you will be able to recognize when you should use the word "no" yourself. Tenacity is not only about holding firm on your position but also being prepared to be persistent where you deem it appropriate; to employ **the "broken record" tactic**. This is a tactic to employ when you need to repeat your position time after time until it registers.

People appreciate things which are difficult to attain. To this end, you should regard most things in negotiation as being difficult, yet possible.

Tenacity is about having the courage of your convictions when faced with challenges from the other party which are often used tactically to make you question your own judgement.

The *Collins English Dictionary* defines tenacity as being persistent and stubborn and to some extent (where appropriate) these qualities serve negotiators well, even though they may not come naturally. You need to be as tenacious in tough Hard Bargaining 4 o'clock deals as you do in more extensive Partnership Agreements at 11 o'clock. Tenacity helps negotiators to work on deals rather than being driven to close on them and conclude agreements prematurely. The more time invested in a deal the more likely you are to create or extract value from it. Few people genuinely enjoy negotiating or can

**CASE STUDY**

The office security alarm salesman was busy selling his latest wireless system to the office facilities manager who had just recently been tasked with protecting a new part of the building he had just taken responsibility for. The facilities manager had two weeks to install a new system and had called in the company responsible for servicing the main building. It had to link to the existing main control box used to manage the main building and be able to link to the fire sprinkler system. All of these were possible and for the alarm company it represented a straightforward job. However, the salesman indicated that the requested two-week time line would not be possible and that he would need to introduce other colleagues, if the sprinkler system connection feature was required. The facilities manager had not built any other options and so was under pressure to make this relationship work. The facilities manager became more flustered as the meeting unfolded when it appeared that he would not be able to deliver on his internal obligations. The account manager held steady and concluded the meeting with a commitment to look into things and report back with some options within 24 hours. Had he sought to conclude the deal there and then no doubt a negotiation over terms would have followed. The next day he called back, and declared that he was able to meet the time lines required following some internal conversations. As a result, he secured list prices on all items and concluded the deal with a relieved and appreciative facilities manager.

see the value in continuing discussions when the deal is seemingly done. Attitudes such as: "We have reached agreement so let's agree now while we're ahead" are held by those who miss the point. It is at this time that "how else can we ensure the contract is delivered?" should be asked. With ever more considerations around how the deal can be tuned, the tenacious negotiator will find the extra value which would otherwise go untouched.

Tenacity helps you to resist capitulation: it's the part of you which enables you to hold your position and not be worn down by the other party. It's an attitude that requires stamina, helping you to seek value right up until you finally agree to conclude the deal.

### 4. ASSERTIVENESS:

#### Tell them what you will do, not what you won't do

The best way to predict the future is to create it.

Being in control of the negotiation primarily comes from being proactive, and demonstrating confidence from being prepared and having a well-defined strategy. Equally, it is about how you perform around the table.

The Complete Skilled Negotiator comes across as being firm and in control. Not obnoxious or disrespectful but simply able to say that which is necessary in an authoritative manner. The credibility this brings in itself attracts respect and suggests through the style of delivery validity of the proposal. This is not about being parental or patronizing in your communication style, but simply confident in your assertions.

This can be a fine line to tread. As an assertive negotiator you need to facilitate the development of the agenda and set out your position, effectively creating an anchor from which the other party has to move you. You should focus on the deal and remain open about what is, as well as what is not, possible. Your motive for outlining to the other party the consequences of no agreement, whilst recognizing your motive for doing so, is not to deadlock the deal, but to posture a position with assertion.

It is worth considering that the outcome of any negotiation can only be influenced by the proposals that you make. Therefore ensure that it is you who is making the proposals. As an assertive negotiator, you will not wait for the other party to make their proposals first. Yes, of course listen to what they have to say to understand where flexibility exists, but ensure that it is your proposal that they are responding to.

As an assertive negotiator you should also resist the temptation to conform. You should regard yourself as being "in charge" but not become so arrogant that you lose touch with the attitudes, feelings and views of those you are negotiating with. Being assertive helps you gain respect. Being firm is not to be confused with being rude.

## 5. INSTINCT:

### Trust it, you will be more often right than not

Experience and "gut feeling" or what some refer to as a "sixth sense" is a trait which effective negotiators refer to as instinct. Instinct helps the Complete Skilled Negotiator to:

- hear not just what is being said but the *meaning* behind the words; and
- gauge honesty, and sense if the deal is too good to be true or if there is more scope to negotiate.

Your ability to read any situation will allow you to judge your response and respond with counter proposals. If it seems too good to be true, it usually is and you should trust your instinct when you are faced with such a situation.

Most people have good instincts, yet under pressure do not always listen to them. They choose instead to accept the case placed before them and conform rather than challenge. As an effective negotiator you should have the courage of your convictions, challenge anything that does not "feel" right, and always demand clarity before being prepared to progress.

Instinct also helps you to weigh up questions such as, are their motives consistent with their behavior? In other words, they are the questions you ask of yourself and your team about how you see the situation, based not only on the numbers alone, but also from experience. For instance, when negotiating in Partnership at 11 o'clock, observations around trust and the sustainability of the relationship will be made up of the views you form from your own instinct.

Ask yourself, "do I think I can make the relationship work? If not, what compensation might I need to accept the risk/compromise of working with them?" This broader perspective is how an economist might consider the situation. However, in some cases, companies have chosen suppliers based on whether the supplier shares similar business values or ethics, rather than purely on the financials. There are some areas of the relationship which may instinctively feel right or wrong.

Trust your instinct, otherwise too narrow a view on the bottom line could ultimately provide you with a suboptimized agreement. Price can be incredibly seductive, and those who shut out other considerations, even when the opportunity feels too good to be true, fall foul of listening to and acting on their instinct. The very need to feel as though you got a great deal can be enough to distract you from the common sense you might otherwise exercise and can lead to disastrous outcomes. Great deals are only so if they are honored and delivered against. Instinctively, you know if you were offered a cheap Rolex watch in a bar by a stranger that the item is unlikely to be from a reputable source. However, how sure would you be if they were in an office dressed in a suit offering a time share apartment in Panama? Still suspicious? OK, how about the real estate agent from a reputable agency who tells you he can sell your house in under a week if you sign with him today?

Instinct usually comes from both experience *and* knowledge, as well as your subconscious observations. The instant evaluation and judgement most people make when they first meet someone else are based on subtle assessments of non-verbal communication and language. The Complete Skilled Negotiator has the ability to make these assessments more consciously as they deliberately analyze the behaviors of the other party.

## 6. CAUTION:

### If it's too good to be true it probably is

The "action" or interaction, once a negotiation has begun, comes in the form of proposals and counter proposals as the deal starts to take shape.

Picture the high levels of mental energy and the work rate taking place *inside* the heads of two teams of negotiators around the table. Both parties are seeking to create or distribute value in the knowledge that if they are too hasty they may miss an implication and, by being seduced on price, they could be entering into an agreement that could carry more risk in the long term. It is during these critical times when reality checks should take place. This is when patience is needed and time should be taken to calculate what has changed.

## CASE STUDY

A Hong Kong based print company called Zenni Print, specializing in large banner posters, was keen to market their own business at a specialist "central government" conference. They had made many enquiries over a period of six months to the organizers and concluded that the fee rate of $10,000 for a space at the site was too expensive; so they decided not to attend. Two weeks before the conference was due to take place, they received a call from a sales representative of the conference organizers who was able to offer Zenni Print a similar size site at the conference for $4500 if they were able to provide an immediate commitment. The Zenni Print director held a short discussion with his team, made a decision to take the slot and returned the call confirming their place. On the day they arrived they were allocated a position outside the main hall, away from where the majority of the people traffic flow existed, and not the premium position they had discussed earlier in the year. They needed to order in additional cabling because the mains power and satellite reception connections were 100 yards away from their site. There was also poor air conditioning in the area which made working on their stand for any period of time too hot and uncomfortable. Their reaction to an offer which seemed too good to be true was lax – they got a good price but did not investigate the implications of the poor deal that followed.

## 7. CURIOSITY:

### Asking why because you want and need to know

In negotiation there is no place for complacency.

Questioning and qualifying in your quest for clarity and understanding are what come more naturally with the trait of curiosity. For some, curiosity comes as naturally as it does to children who, keen to understand the world in which they live, are always asking questions. Gathering information both prior to, and during, the negotiation is the ultimate way of creating power. Even if you think you understand your market well or you have dealt with someone for many years it's still possible to assume far too much. Some negotiators get caught up with what they need to achieve and the pressures they face rather than seeking to understand what the other party needs or how things may have changed for them in recent times. Effective questioning used to seek information and uncover facts, data and circumstances, which may be not be obvious or may even be concealed, *must* be a precursor to making any proposal.

- What are their priorities and why?
- What are their time pressures and why?
- What are their options and why?
- How might any of these be changed?

Understanding the situation does not just come from questioning. Researching the other party, talking to others and obtaining credit checks are activities those who want to know and those who are naturally curious will be involved in. It's not an interrogation, but information is power and without insight you will be a weaker negotiator.

**CASE STUDY**

In the classic Arthur Miller play, *The Price*, which opened on Broadway in 1968, Victor, a New York cop nearing retirement, moves among furniture in the disused attic of a house marked for demolition. Cabinets, desks, a damaged harp, an overstuffed armchair – the relics of a lost life of affluence he's finally come to sell. His attempts to sell are duly rewarded, but not until he has understood the circumstances of the buyer. He repeatedly states: "How can I give you a price if I don't even know who you are, tell me, why do you need it?" The story behind this play sees the price increase many times over from the buyer's opening position as the true value of the furniture becomes evident and the patience and curiosity of the seller pays off. Those who get drawn into dealing too early, or who lack patience, are those who are more likely to make unnecessary compromises.

## 8. NUMERICAL REASONING:

### Know what it's really worth, know what it really costs

Numerical reasoning allows you to consider more easily the "what ifs." Your ability to engineer different trade off scenarios by performing quick calculations allows you to expose opportunities that might otherwise go unnoticed. This involves linking the value of a risk with the benefit of an opportunity by calculating the incremental upside and then tabling it as a proposal. Although it's a good idea to prepare some proposals ahead of your meeting (following initial discussions), calculating counter proposals and providing alternative solutions during the negotiation with similar or even improved outcomes will come more naturally to those comfortable with numerical reasoning.

Unfortunately, for many, this is not the case. Using simple "ready reckoners" to work out the financial implications of movement is one way of preparing yourself for this. For example, working out the implications of each 1% discount or one-week extension, or each 500 increase in unit volume requirements, and having this prepared on a spreadsheet can help you calculate quickly and respond to proposals with a clear understanding of the units and values involved.

**CASE STUDY**

A friend of mine, a fitness fanatic, recently decided to buy himself a multi-gym so that he could work out at home. He conducted his research online and opted to buy a home multi-gym costing him €550. Delivery was "free" and the item would be delivered within 48 hours to his home. He decided to call the retailer first, because he had a few questions about the exercises that the multi-gym would allow him to do. His queries were answered and he placed his order. Before finishing the call, the sales person offered an extra service: "For an extra €170 we will set the machine up for you, should I book this service in for you?" The law of relativity had an immediate effect on his decision making: "€170! The machine is only €550. No I'll be OK, I'll do it myself." Although €170 appeared to be a lot of money, it turned out to be worth more than his entire weekend, because that's how long it took him to construct the giant 288 piece set. Understanding time and value and the total cost of your decisions in any negotiation is critical. However, had the item been offered for €720 including set-up I wonder if he would have bought it?

Numerical reasoning helps you to calculate options or consequences and prepare and be ready to respond with possible alternatives. It helps discussions and ideas to flow and also minimizes the number of times the meeting has to adjourn while one party reworks their figures. If you are in doubt, it's highly appropriate to adjourn. If you are ever in doubt about how the value of the deal has or will change as a result of a proposal, you should take whatever time is necessary to understand the implications of entertaining the proposal before moving on.

### 9. CREATIVITY:

#### Exploring and building on possibilities

Creative solutions not only help resolve deadlock situations but help us to trade off ideas as part of creating more value. By using a creative approach you can link and package variables (volume, timing, specification, etc.) in different ways. Nothing is agreed until everything is agreed so the creative negotiator is comfortable with degrees of ambiguity as the shape of the deal evolves. It provides you with the chance to introduce options and opportunities rather than trying to work through only those issues in front of you in a disciplined, linear fashion.

Many negotiations involve a broad range of variables and the way these are linked together and are traded against each other provides for the art of creative deal-making. Even when it appears that there are few variables, let's say price, timing and specification, the creative negotiator will identify other value-adding considerations and turn them into variables ready for negotiation.

Imagine you are buying 50 acres of land from a farmer. The price asked for the land will be important and transparent to both parties. The timing of the availability of the field will allow you to plan out how you intend to make use of the space. Other considerations may include access to the land, fencing and what the land has been used for in the past. However, the creative negotiator will look at an even broader set of variables as they consider the possible trade-offs. What about options in the future on adjoining land, drainage, conditions on how the surrounding land may be used, and contamination? What about letting the land back to the farmer, and access for local huntsmen that the farmer is involved with and so on?

The creative negotiator examines risk, longevity, performance and the interests of the other party to "fully" scope the parameters of the lifetime of an agreement. The creative negotiator also looks beyond the variables that he or she is measured on as they realize that incremental value may come from elsewhere and often not all components are visible at the outset.

### 10. HUMILITY:

#### It is people who make agreements and humility which breeds respect

Exercising diplomacy and empathy during negotiations to help manage the appropriate climate sounds like common sense. However, with the tensions that exist in negotiations, it's humility that often serves to bring discussions to an adult-to-adult level, cutting through the tactics and gamesmanship in play. Humility removes the need for ego to feature and helps us to demonstrate our intention of working with the other party, rather than against them, to create a mutually beneficial relationship. Reciprocity ensures that if one party becomes competitive, the other party will mirror this behavior and, as a result, both will find themselves being drawn into positional arguments that become counterproductive. It is the

Complete Skilled Negotiator's humility which will allow the other party to "win" the argument as they concentrate on the climate and maximizing the total value of the deal from their perspective.

Ultimately, it is not you who is important; it is what is best for the relationship and for the agreement. It's not about competing or about how you feel. Humility requires the removal of personal emotional considerations other than the need to maintain mutual respect with your focus on the agreement. The skills associated with managing climate are well documented under behaviors later in the next chapter. Humility is what sits beneath the behavior. It is a trait which allows you as a negotiator to focus on the quality of the agreement rather than being preoccupied with personalities and personal agendas.

Although it carries risks, having the confidence to admit that you don't know something (where your credibility would not be completely ruined), being open to ideas without appearing influenced, and making the other party feel important are all indicators of humility in play. It's alright not to know all the answers. It is

**CASE STUDY**

James is a chief negotiator who works in the oil industry. An oil company secured a permit to drill for oil in Hobbs, New Mexico, in 1997 and were successful in unearthing a well. They still had to agree terms with the state of New Mexico for drilling rights. The well was in an area populated by Native American Pima Indians who had significant legal rights in this protected area. At the time, the oil company happened to be involved in discussions with Quest, a large oil refinery company who had extensive experience of building agreements in the state. However, first of all, the oil company needed to agree terms with the Native

American Indians, allowing them to lay pipes across 300 miles of their agricultural land.

The Native Americans obviously wanted as much money as possible for the agreement. The agreement was for ten years and stood to transform the area and their own wealth. However, the oil company had assumed that the price would hold the key to agreement. The parties involved in the negotiation demonstrated little respect for each other and after six months of discussions, negotiations ground to a halt.

Quest, who had an interest in acquiring a refinery contract in the event that the agreement progressed, also had significant local experience and offered to help out. Many of their negotiators had first-hand experience of working with the Pima Indians. It turned out that respect and confidence and a broader agenda was all that was needed. A range of community investment programmes around education and infrastructure were tabled during discussions. In addition, 50% representation on an advisory board, focused on which route the pipes should take, was offered to the tribe leaders. It took two weeks for the deal to be concluded, which in itself changed the dynamics of the negotiation that followed involving Quest and the oil company.

The Indians needed to trust their partners and wanted to be involved.

James described this to me, once the deal had been completed, saying that "nobody will concede or give you better terms because they like you but there are plenty that will not do business because they take a disliking to you," which still remains with me 14 years after having witnessed this 12 o'clock partnership-dependent negotiation.

knowing what questions to ask and demonstrating integrity and gravitas that allows those with humility to build the appropriate relationship for the more interdependent deals.

## CONCLUSION

Most of us have relative strengths in relation to the ten traits and, by definition, traits can come more or less naturally to us. They serve to promote or constrain our behavior and competence as negotiators. Where behaviors can be developed, traits need to be understood, as it is your self-awareness that will ultimately affect what you do, how you perform and whether you continue to learn and grow from each negotiation you are involved in. If you are not naturally creative or tenacity is not something you are at ease with, this need not be an issue. It is the people who recognize this who become Complete Skilled Negotiators.

# CHAPTER 5

# The Fourteen Behaviors that Make the Difference

The framework for our negotiation standard now starts to unfold. It is time to face yourself and your capability as a negotiator, recognizing the significant difference that a competent performance can make to the bottom line. The clock face has provided the basis for differentiating the many ways to negotiate. The role of power helps us understand how situations and relationships can be manipulated or influenced, meaning that we have to continuously reassess our assumptions. The ten negotiation traits we examined in Chapter 4 provide a framework for self-awareness, enabling us to do that which is appropriate. In this chapter I present the fourteen behaviors which enable you to do the right thing at the right time. Together, the traits and behaviors support the competent performance of the Complete Skilled Negotiator.

## YOUR BEHAVIORS AND ATTRIBUTES

The great thing about behaviors in negotiation is that they can be developed. Are negotiators born or made? It's fair to say that we each have traits which lend themselves better to some skills than others. However, effective negotiation is an output of what you do and this is why developing these fourteen behaviors is fundamental to your ability and performances as a negotiator.

Consider any professional sports player who needs a range of skills to perform at the highest level. For example, a tennis professional needs to be able to serve, gauge the second serve, lob, backhand top spin, smash at the net, forearm top spin, slice, forearm back spin and so on. The range of skills required makes up their total game and their ability to deal with different types of situations. The same can be said for golfers, Formula One drivers, basketball players, and indeed anyone who needs to perform in competitive, changing environments.

Another interesting parallel between sports pros and negotiators is coaching and preparation. Sports pros have their own coaches. Training is a constant feature of their lives if they are to compete at the top. There are similar challenges for negotiators who are ultimately measured by the success of the outcomes of their deals. Those who believe that their position of strength requires little preparation, or that the skills they have developed over the years will continue to serve them well in the future, are in denial. Regardless of the type of agreement you may be involved in, the amount of time people actually spend negotiating is relatively small compared with all other aspects of conducting business. When you add up the number of hours spent actually negotiating around the table, even the largest of deals can be completed within a few days. Most agreements are negotiated in hours or even less.

If you were to divide every minute you spent negotiating by the value at stake in your negotiations you would probably equate your time to be incredibly valuable. Imagine you were negotiating a contract to supply building materials to a contractor and the value for the year is worth $5 million. You become involved in three meetings over the next month to explore a range of issues. In total you spend four hours involved in face-to-face negotiations. The margin opportunity on the deal needs to be protected and you discuss delivery times, ordering processes and a range of other variables. The potential profitability of the deal to you is likely to be $1 million, 20% of the total value. During the course of negotiations as you discuss terms the profitability of the agreement fluctuates as you work through variables, including payment scheduling, discounting and others. The profitability of the deal also fluctuates depending on what is agreed, much of which will be down to your performance. Let's say your performance results in you influencing the outcome by 15%. So there is $150,000 at stake depending on your performance divided by the four hours of negotiations you have invested. That's $37,500 an hour depending on your performance or $625 a minute!

The skill of negotiating probably offers the opportunity to create more value per minute invested than any other skill you may use in your job. Now imagine the deal was worth $1 billion. How much would your time be worth now? That is why negotiators, like top sports pros, need to reappraise their skills and retrain on an ongoing basis.

### *Defining what you do in negotiation*

The fourteen negotiation behaviors capture and describe what it is that you do when negotiating. They make up the varied skills required to perform at different points on the clock face and allow you to be versatile enough to perform in all types of situations. They have been used as a framework for assessing, developing and supporting negotiations in over 500 corporate businesses around the globe for more than a decade, employing the clock face as their "standard" negotiation reference.

**The first five behaviors** are more commonly, although not exclusively, used on the right-hand side of the clock face (1–6 o'clock negotiations), yet can also underpin those behaviors further around the clock face.

**The next three behaviors** are based on listening, planning and questioning, and relate to all points on the clock face.

**The final six behaviors**, which build on the former behaviors, help us to perform in more complex deals where relationship, dependency, and total value are more important.

Although most businesses involved in business-to-business (B2B) negotiations like to think that their negotiations take place on the left-hand side of the clock face (more collaborative), the reality is that few negotiations stick to any one position for the entire negotiation. In fact, all negotiators need *all* of the behaviors if they are to be versatile, adaptable and ultimately secure good deals.

**CASE STUDY**

The national account manager of a South African IT outsourcing service business arranged a meeting with his largest customer to discuss the performance of the account. He also planned to discuss areas for improvement and to kick off discussions relating to trading terms between them for the following year. He believed the account had performed well, that service levels had been achieved and that the relationship was in a good position to move forward. He worked for Sedex Serve, a company that prided itself on highly collaborative relationships with clients and long-term agreements. The manager had finely tuned interpersonal skills and charm that had suited Sedex Serve and the major accounts he managed. On his way to the meeting, he received a call from his client informing him that his main client contact (the IT controller) had called in sick and would not be able to make the meeting. The IT director, however, was available to take the meeting, which the account manager agreed to.

Within moments of the meeting commencing, the IT director launched into a set of demands for discounts, innovations and performance improvements together with deadlines and ultimatums. He said that the account had been underinvested in and had become a cash cow for Sedex Serve. He also made an allegation that poor service levels had resulted in the business losing its competitive edge.

The account manager took the feedback and attempted to reassure the director. He felt obligated to respond and did so with everything he had at his disposal. He committed to extra resources, quicker response times, a 15% loyalty discount and even an extension to payment terms. Pressure, the risk implication and the fact that the director was empowered to terminate the account resulted in a total capitulation. Now this was an intelligent and experienced national account manager who prided himself on negotiating good agreements. He had rarely been exposed to tough demanding environments like this. He did not see it coming and so was unprepared and unable to adapt to the pressured environment. Ultimately, he failed to maintain his composure, take notes or adjourn the meeting. He simply caved in. His performance lost him respect and it lost Sedex Serve $2 million a year in profit on the account.

The experience in this case may not be a regular occurrence for most managers. However, it's one of many illustrations I have come across where empowered managers without all the skills necessary to handle all situations around the clock face and at some time or another find themselves in a compromised position.

The left-hand side of the clock face is where the greatest value opportunity lies. It's a more challenging environment because negotiations here rely more heavily on relationships and the agreements built tend to be made up of a broader range of variables. The opportunity for future business will exist, which promotes mutual dependency, and the need for at least some level of trust and collaboration.

However, the world is not always a rational place and just because there is dependency between those involved does not mean that cooperation will follow. Power does unpredictable things to people and organizations. In all types of negotiation it is people's egos that can make for incredibly competitive environments, which is why we need to understand and master all aspects of negotiation if we are to build sustainable agreements.

## THE FOURTEEN BEHAVIORS

### *1. Think clearly when faced with conflict*

Everything you do in negotiation requires you to think: if you can't think clearly your performance is going to be compromised. In some ways, it is similar in its definition to the personal trait of nerve (see page 105, Chapter 4). The extent of conflict, real or perceived, within a negotiation will vary depending on the strategy being adopted by both parties. The ability to think clearly when faced with conflict is one that will serve any negotiator well at any point on the clock face.

When involved in hard bargaining negotiations (4 o'clock), keeping a clear head and remaining focused on the deal without allowing their positioning to distract your focus or thinking can be difficult.

Yet it is this very skill that will help you to respond appropriately. How can you examine options, think creatively, or even build a collaborative climate, if you are emotionally constrained by the fact that the other party has just put what you think is a ridiculously low opening offer on the table? To walk away would be like a boxer knocked down once and not picking himself up. You have to gather your thoughts and remove any emotion from your thinking, without which you will lose composure and more likely under perform.

Thinking clearly also involves clarity of thought; not allowing the other party to make you feel as though it is you who does not understand the market and who needs to move. If you are not sure about the deal or what it adds up to, then get out. You can always return to the table once you have taken time to consider your options. Never agree to anything unless you understand it. In negotiation, nothing is agreed until everything is agreed, so make sure you have not missed anything before agreeing.

Thinking clearly when faced with conflicting positions also means standing up to anyone exercising arrogance as they attempt to manipulate your thinking – unless you want them to think they are doing so because it serves your interests. See the arrogance or irrationality for what it is and control the negotiation by restating your position and letting them do the talking. You may find it uncomfortable but it will gain you respect and you won't find yourself in a position of regret after the deal because of what you "allowed to happen."

You can control the negotiation only if you remain clear in thought. Demand clarity as a condition of continuing. Control the pace of the meetings through the questions you ask, slowing the process down and making your **power statement** for them to

**power statement**
This is a statement made that is implied as a fact which suggests high dependency on their part.

think about. For example, "I understand you have to sell by the end of the month?" Their reaction will be one of denial, confirmation or justification. Any of these will provide you with insights and will ensure that it is you who is controlling the meeting.

When there are major consequences at stake, or serious time pressures in play and there is an obligation on you to perform, you will experience pressure. Depending on how much pressure, your ability to think clearly may be affected. It's your ability to cope with this that will differentiate your performance, especially in hard bargaining negotiations. Thinking clearly also involves remaining focused on your purpose. It is the first behavior without which all other skills will be compromised.

### 2. *Do not allow your sense of fairness to influence behavior*

This is the most contentious or most easily misunderstood of behaviors, and yet provides a genuine reality check for anyone believing that we are all the same or have the same power, the same ethics, or the same motives.

The negotiation process is just that, a process, and as such needs to be controlled and managed. If everyone were open and fair there would be no need to negotiate.

Fairness has no place in negotiation. Being focused on your purpose in negotiation requires a mindset that can't be distorted by a desire to be fair. We are all conditioned to some extent by our values upon which we lead our lives. Both social and business values include being fair. Even politicians talk about "a fairer society." But you can't objectively measure fair in negotiations. What's fair to you may not seem fair to the other party so it cannot be relied on as a basis for seeking agreement.

However, the perception of fairness is important where you need balanced cooperation with the other party and where you need to work with them on an ongoing basis. But "fair" is a subjective word and a relative term. You offer one person a price of $40 and they think that's a fair price. You offer another person a price of $40 and they think it's unfair. The first has been used to paying $45 elsewhere and thinks they have a good deal and the price is fair. The second has never purchased before but is expecting a price of $35, so is not happy. Relativity can be seen in all areas of negotiation: a price increase, changes in other terms, or when a workers' union is renegotiating on the fairness of proposed changes for its members.

### Splitting the difference?

Capitalism is not designed to be fair, although most people naively expect it to be so. It may sound harsh but few things are fair in life and rarely does anyone get what they deserve. You get what you negotiate. In negotiation, if you expect the market pressures to be fair then you will be disappointed and if you set out to be fair, for no other reason than it's how you like to do business with others, then you will pay for it. However, in some lines of business fairness towards the other party that you know will be reciprocated can be critical to gaining and maintaining trust. This is not to suggest that you should act unfairly. Rather, you should not allow your sense of fairness to dominate your thinking.

Fairness is not the answer to conflict. Opting to split differences straight down the middle, for example, each time you are faced with difference is not negotiating: it is compromising. If they offer to split down the middle, it usually means that the middle position is one they are prepared to accept and that they would probably accept less if pushed. Importantly, rather than grabbing the deal with the final 50:50 split, why not offer a further conditional proposal which costs you less than 50% of the difference? The need to exhibit fairness often leads inexperienced negotiators to accept the 50:50 offer. This is because it feels "fair," when they should make further counter proposals to provide less costly solutions.

Maximizing profit need not mean it's to the detriment of the other party; meaning because you get more out of the deal that they should get less. Being able to put fairness to one side simply allows us to focus on other skills, rather than opting for an easy route involving an unnecessary concession which we justify as being the fair thing to do. Negotiation is and should be hard work and rewarding. The easy, fair route to splitting the difference is rarely the optimum way to the best deal for all concerned.

### Keeping your values

Control, awareness and doing things which, although uncomfortable, are necessary in negotiation come from understanding the role of fairness when agreeing terms. Understanding and accommodating the emotional pressures we face in negotiation helps us to respond by looking for the optimum solution rather than simply a fair one. Effective negotiation does not require you to change your values as they present a framework for your life – only to help you to understand how they will influence your feelings, emotions, behavior and performance during your negotiations.

The more you try to be fair, the more your "generosity" will be taken advantage of. If you give a little, they will take a lot, so all trade-offs should be conditional. Most people will not live by the same value set as you. They may need the business more or may simply be more callous or irrational about how they go about trading. One thing is for sure, they are out to maximize profit and, if you make it easy for them, it will be to the detriment of your position.

Perversely, people who do operate in a fair way during negotiations can in fact be perceived as unfair. For example, in a hard bargaining situation at 4 o'clock someone may decide not to ask for more than they expect in the first instance and provide an opening position that is reasonable as (see page 41, Chapter 2): they do not want to offend the other party. Their sense of fairness results in them feeling uncomfortable with the prospect of rejection, which would be likely in the event of them opening with a very high or low offer. The other party, however, expecting to negotiate, will want them to move from their opening position in order to gain some satisfaction. They have two options: either to give away value that they cannot afford to (because they have already opened on their break point); or they have to say "no" and not move. This in itself could lead to a perception of stubbornness, unfairness and, potentially, deadlock.

Firm is not rude, tough is not nasty. Liked is not respected. When hard bargaining, nice people don't get good deals.

### 3. *Maintain your self-control, use silence and manage discomfort*

During a hard bargaining negotiation at 4 o'clock, there is inevitably a conflict in positions: "What you get, I lose, and what I get, you lose." It is a zero sum game. For example, as a result of the opening positions taken up being at different extremes and with few issues to negotiate around, the opening positions are rejected. What usually follows is tension and sometimes even emotion. This reaction is sometimes orchestrated or can be a natural outburst.

Self-control allows you to exercise:

- nerve
- intransigence
- rejection.

These behaviors could be described as arrogant, and uncooperative. This competitive behavior might otherwise be regarded as unacceptable in many relationships, if used outside of the context of hard bargaining negotiation, but when you are trying to move the other person's position, self-control and silence are the most powerful of behaviors to conduct. Negotiation has less to do with talking and more to do with listening. The reason you listen is to understand what they are saying to you as you seek to establish how far they will move from their current position. You should let the other party:

- sell their position;
- explain their position;
- promote all the benefits; and
- explain why they need an agreement "today."

"Today did you say?" At which point you make them an extreme, yet realistic, offer aimed at adjusting their expectations. Negotiation is silence and to master this is to maintain self-control and manage the resulting discomfort. You can't think (behavior 1: think clearly) and talk at the same time without losing some control over the message you are trying to get across. If you are not ready to make your proposal, either ask a question or say nothing. Information is power and the more they talk the more powerful you will become.

- Let them do the talking.
- Focus your attention first on what they are saying, rather than thinking too much about how you should respond.

It's a simple process that many people struggle with because it feels uncomfortable and goes against our social values of wanting to be accommodating or wanting to be liked.

### *4. Open extreme yet realistically to shift their expectations*

#### How to open with an extreme position

To open extreme is simple enough, as you just state your proposal. The fear of the predictable rejection, however, results in many feeling uncomfortable with stating it in the first place. Because of the fear of the reaction we are expecting, we risk losing our composure. Rather than saying "my price is $50," we end up saying something like, "I'm looking for around $50," which instantly suggests it's negotiable. If it's worth $100 to you, offer $50. We know they are going to reject the offer but that's part of the process.

You can't change or remove this feeling of being uncomfortable so you need to get used to it or find ways to accommodate it. To do this, think about it as a process that you are involved in. The process will do three things for you.

1. Firstly it will help you to position your offer appropriately.
2. Secondly it will help you to counter the position of the other party.
3. Thirdly, it will ensure you provide the other party with the satisfaction of having got a better deal than they believed was originally available.

When the other person remains silent and you feel obliged to respond, don't. Don't pay the price by instantly conceding as you attempt to remove your discomfort, because if you speak too early, that is what will happen. *If you have nothing to say, say nothing.* They are thinking. Let them think. If you speak to fill the gap, you will probably end up compromising your position by offering further information or even by implying that there is room for movement.

In more creative negotiations, self-discipline is critical to avoid giving your position away. Remember, they are out to maximize their position and will often go to extremes to achieve it. Learn to be at ease with silence. Watch the other party and wait for them. Look at them and show them that it is they who have to move first.

In a hard bargaining 4 o'clock negotiation your job is to get agreement on, or as near as you can, to their **break point**. The first activity involved in achieving this is through your opening position, which should be planned and prepared in advance. This will set the foundation of your negotiation. Your opening position or proposal should be extreme enough for them not to accept it, but not so extreme that they choose to walk away, concluding the conversation there and then. If your opening position is too extreme, the other party may conclude that you are wasting their time, are not serious and move on. Your offer also has to be realistic if they are to stay engaged.

**break point**

The point at which the other party will deadlock, walk away or conclude discussions rather than agree; the point at which a better option or BATNA means there is no need to agree.

For example, if you wanted to buy something for $200 and they are asking $300, you might negotiate them down, depending on the circumstances. But if you were attempting to finish at $200 by opening at $25, then they would probably walk away without any further dialogue unless there were some quite incredible circumstances in play. It's just too far away for it to have any relation to their expectations. Extreme and yet realistic openers are designed to impact on expectations but if the other party feel patronized or insulted it usually presents a real risk of them just walking away from the discussion. Of course this is highly dependent on circumstances but if you were to open with an offer of $105, moving to $135, then $150 and a final offer of $155; in relative terms this will feel to the other party a whole lot more realistic, although at first unappealing. Of course, all will depend on their circumstances as you read them.

Your position should provide you with room to move as you test their response but not be so extreme that you wreck any chance of dialogue, without which there is no chance of an agreement of any sort. The purpose of opening extreme is to create an anchor from which to move. If you have control over your own sense of fairness and can manage your discomfort, then you will be able to do this. Assuming the other party is still talking to you, you are now in a proactive position which allows movement on your part, given that you will have taken up an opening position outside of their break point.

Of course, the opening position has to be realistic otherwise you will lose any cooperation and they may regard you as not credible and will conclude the conversation there and then. So you need to gauge a position which is unacceptable and yet not beyond their emotional need to reject or to the point where they leave. This involves:

- applying self-control when making your offer; and
- stating your figure and shutting up.

The firmness of your figure or proposal will further ensure the other party continues to reassess their position. Remember to make your position credible by cutting out any soft exposing statements: avoid the use of words like "around," "in the region of," "I was hoping for...," "we were expecting..." Selling or justifying your position will also only serve to undermine it.

A non-verbal reaction to their opening position tactically known as the **professional flinch** is designed to clearly demonstrate to the other party your surprise at their position. Being physical rather than verbal it is a much stronger way of affecting their aspirations. Your expression will say more than the words can. However, laughing at their figure is both predictable and can easily antagonize.

**professional flinch**
A non-verbal reaction to the other party's opening position.

You can wipe their extreme openers off the table by attaching equally ludicrous conditions to their price. Imagine a seller said to you "the price is $150." You respond with: "I can agree, subject to payment installments over three years and that the item is guaranteed for the duration of the payment plan." In negotiation you never need to say no. You can always re engineer the variables in such a way that you can say yes and yet attract improved terms. Simply attach conditions which offset the implications of saying yes. Also, you never have to, nor should you, lie in negotiations. There is no need to if you understand the process you are involved in. The process of opening extreme is simply that – a process – and is usually employed in the hard bargaining context. By offering $50 you are not lying, you are simply making an offer by telling them what you will agree to.

During tough one-dimensional negotiations, it is important to recognize that you can get a great price and yet a lousy deal. Never get so into driving their position that you lose sight of other issues that may result in a poor deal. An antique clock collector negotiated an amazingly low price on a clock at an antiques fair. The seller said that it needed "some attention" as it was not working. However, he was seduced by the price he had been able to agree and bought it. That was five years ago. The clock has now been through three different repairs, costing the collector the asking price over again. After each repair the clock worked for less than a week. It now sits at the back of his workshop.

If it appears too good to be true, it usually is.

### 5. *Read their break point*

In any hard bargaining negotiation, you should define your break point first. That is:

- The point at which you have other options that you could take.
- The point at which the deal is not viable.
- The point at which you will walk, rather than do business.

This is not your objective or a measure, just a fail-safe position. Its only purpose is to prevent you from agreeing to a deal which in the cold light of day is just not viable. Your job when hard bargaining is to finish the deal as close to their break point as possible. So therefore, your first task is to work out where you think this is, and then open extreme and yet realistic on the other side of it. They will not be able to agree to your offer and will therefore reject it. Expect this, it's OK, it's part of the process. Let them attack it, talk about it, rubbish it, be emotional about your apparent irrationality. The more they do, the stronger your anchor becomes because they are already thinking about how they can move you to a position that they can accept.

When operating at 4 o'clock, the negotiator's role is to work out the other party's break point and drive them to it. This is the point measured financially or in other terms beyond which they will walk away from the offer rather than reluctantly agree. The challenge for any negotiator is working out where this is. Getting into their head to identify their break-point position can be one of the more instinctive tasks of a negotiator (thus making use of trait 5, instinct, page 111). However, instinct is also knowing how far to push them, as every individual has different emotional thresholds. The untrained negotiator will probably not even have a break point of their own and because of this will make spur-of-the-moment decisions based on what they are prepared to accept.

Reading their break point is about reading the situation based on a combination of information, questioning, and reading of their actions. All should help you to establish how much they need the deal and how far they will go. Time can play a role here. Where negotiations go on for weeks and months, many will agree to offers that would have been totally unacceptable during the earlier stages of the negotiation. Sometimes the negotiation process serves to wear them down; it could be that other options they thought they had have dissolved or that the time and energy spent negotiating would be better spent elsewhere, so they conclude the deal. Sometimes circumstances change over the duration of the negotiation, throwing up more options or alternatives and therefore influencing the flow of events.

Under great pressure some have even been known to capitulate and forget their break point altogether. How many times have you heard of people who have come out of an auction having paid far more than the limit they had set themselves because they got caught up in the heat of the moment?

You can read the other party's limits through:

- the types of proposals they make;
- the language they use to justify their movements;
- the timescales they are working to; and
- the size and frequency of their concessions or counter proposals.

This will help you to identify their break point. Their opening position and response to yours will help you plot where you think they may settle. Under pressure people often say (without realizing) the exact opposite of what they actually mean to say. For example if they say "we once paid $60 an hour for this and would not do it again" they are saying this not to you but to themselves. And, even *they* do not believe it. It's their denial which drives this behavior so listen to what they are saying. If they were not prepared to go to $60 an hour they would not feel the need to state it.

Often, they will tell you they are indifferent to your proposal and demand that you improve your offer. They will say that they have other options and may even sound quite believable. It is the way you *question to qualify* what they are saying, and the answers or reasons you attract, which is where the true insights start to appear (see page 147, behavior 8, Question effectively).

### Defining your own break point

Defining your break point can be done by working out what is your best alternative in the event that your negotiation breaks down. Your Best Alternative to a Negotiated Agreement (BATNA) is one way of working out your break point. Another could be "timing," in that you might prefer to wait for the market to improve, for circumstances to change to strengthen your position, assuming you are not facing time pressures. For the other party, market conditions, competitor activity and other suppliers, or customers they may have, will help them form their own BATNA assuming they are so inclined. You can also assess where their break point is by examining previous agreements where you have dealt with them before. You can research the market, speak to their competitors, and ultimately predict at what point they are most likely to walk away from the deal.

### Identifying issues

Remember you are negotiating with a person, not a company. They will carry a set of circumstances which will be unique to them. Timescales, availability, quantity, convenience, timing and so on, will all have a bearing on what they will or can accept today. Even this may be different from yesterday based on changing circumstances. When dealing with a range of negotiation variables, set out to understand the value of each issue from their perspective. Identify how sensitive or susceptible they are to ideas around each issue.

Identify the issues of high value to them. Try to establish those issues on which they are prepared to be more flexible, as part of building a more accurate picture of where their break point is. You can identify these by reading their reaction to suggestions. You can also test your own assumptions by stating them as facts and waiting for their response.

### *6. Listen and interpret the meaning behind the words*

Watch them, watch for **the signals**. This can include phrases such as "well that wasn't as much as we were hoping for" or "I can't go that far" or "I was looking for a higher figure," all of which suggest they are in the process of revising their expectations.

As a Complete Skilled Negotiator, understanding their position, priorities, interests, pressures and needs is a critical part of your job. It's these things that will have the most influence on the value they have placed on the issues you are about to negotiate.

**the signals**

What the other party says or does, and what this means in the context of the discussion.

Information is power and this is one sure way of building power: by listening and interpreting their true position. How much do they need this deal? How many options do they really have? How dependent are they on an early decision? There is so much to be learnt through what we see and hear. The term "getting into their head" has as much to do with getting *out* of our own head. Rather than concentrating on our own thoughts and feelings, we need to consciously turn our attentions to theirs.

Listening to what the other party says is only part of the skill involved in reading and understanding them. Look for inconsistencies in the way they attempt to justify their position. The more they talk, the weaker they are feeling. If they start to sell the benefits of their offer during the negotiation, they are feeling weak. Remember the same will apply in the way they read your behavior.

- **Establish how firm their offer or proposal is.** Try to observe the "soft exposing giveaways": "I was looking for around $500, if that sounds OK?" This is not a firm offer; it's a very obvious example of someone feeling uncomfortable tabling their opening offer. Often we are given less obvious hints, yet there can still be clues within how their proposal is stated. Try to listen for what is said and how it is said. The value of listening is far greater than that which can be achieved by what you have to say.
- **Another area to focus on is listening to the questions asked.** For example, if they ask you if it is available today, or if you can pay cash, rather than simply answering those questions, you should think about *why* they are asking such a question, and perhaps ask in return why this is important to them. If you are wrapped up in your own head, then you will miss the opportunity to qualify the things which are important to them.
- **Once you have listened, stop and interpret what the information offers.** This should be before you feel obliged to respond. For many, the time taken feels uncomfortable, but the new information needs time to be considered. If they are selling and are opening with $500, where might their break point be? Think about this before you respond. The ability to actively listen for information which may help progress the negotiation, rather than using the time available to think about what you want to say next, leans heavily on the negotiator's trait of curiosity (trait 7, page 115, Chapter 4).

The temptation to talk when the pressure is on or when there is silence is, for many, overpowering. Your ability to resist this will play a key part in your negotiation armory. Learn to shut up and speak only when you have something considered to say, or you are ready to move proceedings along – always consciously and with intent.

### *7. Plan and prepare using all information available*

There is a direct correlation between successful negotiations, however measured, and the time invested in preparation. Planning can be as simple as building an agenda or as complex as managing many stakeholders involved in multiple negotiations around the world requiring a detailed strategy and tactical analysis for all concerned. It is important to emphasize just how critical planning is as a discipline and as a behavior as so few managers plan properly, taking the attitude that they can still perform without it. This is explored in greater depth in the final chapter of this book.

The Complete Skilled Negotiator recognizes that this is the one discipline that you ignore at your peril. Insight, options, confidence, direction, knowledge and control can all be gained from preparation using all information available. Negotiators should never "wing it" and, for so many, egos get in the way. This results in an attitude of familiarity with the situation or relationship which results in no or poor quality preparation. We all work under pressure and the task of planning can often be minimized or even forgotten in favor of "more urgent" tasks. You have to take the time to plan. It has been proven time after time that effective negotiators plan.

They plan:

- what to ask;
- what to open with;

- what operating agenda to use;
- how to open;
- how to respond;
- what information they need;
- when and where the meeting will be held;
- who needs to be involved; and
- when will discussion commence and much more.

The time to start getting into their head is during your preparation. Work out or predict the value of different issues to them and how changing circumstances may affect their perspective on the agreement.

Focus your attention on each variable you are likely to discuss and be precise about the information you need or the questions you plan to ask before your meeting. Don't skip it, do it because it will pay off so many times over.

Keep a record to simplify future planning. Work out who you are going to involve in your negotiation meeting. Involve others in your preparation where you feel they may have something to contribute, allowing them to test your assumptions. Having others involved not only strengthens your discipline to do it, but attracts ideas and approaches which you may not have considered yourself.

Plan the agenda and map out the issues which you can conditionally trade around. Make a point of understanding the unit values involved against each of the variables so that you can be ready to trade. For example, you can start with planning your opening position or reviewing your existing contract arrangements. Scope the issues to help visualize the possible variables and trade-offs, which will, in turn, help your confidence and performance as your meeting gets started.

Some negotiations can take weeks or even months to prepare for. Even routine negotiations should be given as long as necessary to work through the issues, values and possibilities. It provides insight, confidence and structure. All of this will help you take control of your negotiation. Planning as part of the negotiation process should never be ignored or underestimated.

At a strategic level, your planning and preparation should involve the sequencing of events, managing communication across the various stakeholders, working through how to frame your proposals and, depending on your strategy, anchoring your position, which we will cover in more detail in Chapter 9.

### *8. Question effectively*

In March 2007, a senior government official in the UK confessed that his biggest regret was not challenging the assumptions being made about the existence of weapons of mass destruction prior to the invasion of Iraq. He admitted that more questions could have prompted more answers, which may have altered the course of history.

Developing open-ended questions to understand the other party using **STROB** is part of the Complete Skilled Negotiator's approach to ensuring that no stone is left unturned. This structured approach enables you to plan out how you can extract more information than might otherwise be forthcoming.

**STROB**

Scope, Terms, Risks, Options, Barriers.

- **Scope** (*Testing parameters, assumptions and level of empowerment*).
- **Terms** (*Examining their requirements and how they are motivated*).
- **Risks** (*Identifying opportunities to value and distribute risk*).
- **Options** (*Defining their alternatives*).
- **Barriers** (*Predicting objections or sensitive areas which will attract resistance*).

For each of these areas the Complete Skilled Negotiator, as part of their planning, will create five open-ended questions which will help them open up or expand their knowledge and understanding:

1 Examine broadening the **SCOPE** of the agreement as part of broadening or narrowing your relationship. This could include considering the longevity of the relationship, dependency, risk or other factors, which create greater scope for maximizing value.
2 List the **TERMS** you think will feature and their relative value to them. This could include their basic requirements, issues or related to how the individual negotiator will be measured.
3 List any issues they or you may regard as **RISK** related. This could include time scales, third party relationships, market assumptions, etc.
4 List any/all of the **OPTIONS** you believe they may have in the event that your negotiations run into difficulties. In the event of deadlock what would they do?
5 List the potential **BARRIERS**, issues or objections that are likely to be presented.

The STROB technique is used by converting your questions into order of importance, listing your top ten and using these during the exploratory phase of your discussions.

Open, closed, rhetorical and assumptive questions are available as part of your armory. Be careful, though – if you're seen to be interrogating, you're likely to attract suspicion and resistance.

Making use of "what if" questions to establish how the other party might respond to different scenarios and their attitude to risk can also help during your exploratory meetings. They can also be used to help identify priorities and the value the other party places on certain issues. "What if we order 50,000?", "What if we order 100,000?", "So what if we order 600,000 then?" – these are questions which will help you to understand the economies of volume. Taken a step further, you can start to question timings, payment terms and all other variables with "what ifs" to help establish how their cost base is made up, what is easier for them to agree on and where flexibility lies within their list of interests.

So, with planning generally, make a conscious effort to work on the different questioning types. It will help you to maintain control. If you are asking the questions, then you are guiding the discussion without having the obligation of providing them with information. If they are reluctant to answer, try the question in a different way, but be aware, you can sometimes give away your own interests unintentionally by the way you ask questions.

The Complete Skilled Negotiator will have the confidence to be flexible and will use a combination of questioning styles to enable them to extract the most useful information (see below).

QUESTION TYPES

- **Contact questions** help establish rapport: "How have you been since we last met? Did you have a good holiday? How is business?"
- **Probing questions** help to seek further information: "What do you think about your competitor's latest activities?"
- **Interrogative questions** help to encourage them to think about solutions for themselves: "Why is that important to you?"
- **Comparative questions** help to explore in detail: "What has business been like since the introduction of product A? How have things changed since your new promotion began?"
- **Extension questions** to challenge: "How do you mean? How else could we do that? What are you thinking of specifically? What do you mean when you say …? How can you be sure of that?"
- **Opinion seeking questions** to test their knowledge and thinking: "How do you feel about …? What do you think about …? What are your views on …?"
- **Hypothetical questions** which help to test their knowledge and thinking: "What if we were to order 500 units? What if we included all the costs? What if I paid you in advance?"
- **Reflective/summary questions** to draw ideas together and test their understanding, and summarize what has been said: "So, you think that we need to introduce this new range? You think that the product will achieve X? As I understand it, you reckon that you can deliver it?"

- **Closing questions** help to secure agreement: "When should we start – during May or at the beginning of June? I can deliver on the first or second week of that month; which would suit you best? How much?"
- **Mirror questions** serve to reverse the question and confirm the point: "We think we can deliver this for you." "You think you can deliver this?"
- **Leading questions** help to secure a desired answer. "You can't deny that ...? Isn't it a fact that ...? You wouldn't say that ...? It's a great offer, isn't it?"
- **Rhetorical questions** help to prevent them from saying anything: questions which do not require an answer: "Do we really want to do that? And how did that happen?" *Implying that you already know.*
- **Multiple questions** which help to gain agreement to a package: "You did say that you could meet the deadline? Oh, and you will meet our specification and, ah, by the way, you can do this for us can't you?"
- **Closed questions** which help to establish specific facts/information: "Will you do this? Have you the ability to deliver? Can you meet our requirements? Do you need help with this offer?"

### 9. *Always trade concessions effectively and conditionally*

Every trade you make should be considered and conditional.

The aim of trading is to build more value for your business as a result of each trade. As there are no rules in negotiation, you can, in theory, offer anything which has a value to them, providing it is a reciprocated move. Whatever they want, they can have, in return for something you want. Each trade then should be designed to provide you with a net gain. In practice you will of course want to weigh up any variable traded as the implications of trading it may be broader than simply its financial value.

Imagine an international footballer in the transfer market about to move club. The negotiation involves the player's agent and the chairman of the football club. The agenda is made up of a transfer fee, a signing on fee, length of contract, salary and bonuses, and a range of performance-related incentives and obligations the player has to meet. Variables could also include the phasing of payments in relation to appearances, number of goals scored or whether they appear for their country. Each variable will feature as part of a set of conditional trade-offs. The club, having chosen their man, want to ensure that they get maximum value from his services. Meanwhile the player may be looking for maximum income or flexibility within the contract, known as "personal terms." Each of the variables can be adjusted as part of the negotiation which follows and the process involved is that of trading concessions.

When trading concessions you therefore need to identify through your planning and questioning what is important to them. This will help you to build proposals that involve concessions which are the least cost to you, but represent a greater value to them. In return, your condition is that they provide movement which improves the value of the deal for you. This sounds rational, fair and transparent but it's usually not, in that what they offer will be no more than they absolutely have to and usually this is something of a minimum cost to them.

Understanding the implications of their offer is critical if you are to assess what you want in return. Your creativity can work wonders when you move away from price only, and focus on total cost or total value.

Remember always to place your condition first, as they will only hear what they want to hear. If the concession comes first rather than the condition, they may block out anything that follows it. This can be framed as:

"If you … then we …"

You are also less likely to be interrupted as they have not heard what is in it for them yet.

### Trading concessions and conditions using the right questions

Again, you can explore trades by using "what if" questions. For instance, "What if we offered you a more flexible start date? Would that help you to meet the manpower requirements?" You are not offering it, merely exploring the value and measuring their reaction to the suggestion. If they state that they would accept it, you can then make it conditional on a further concession which you would expect.

Try to be creative when identifying options for trading. Changing the shape of the deal can often help. You can simply ask them "What would help you?" or "How could I make this deal more profitable for you?" It sounds obvious, but again so many get caught up in competing on positions or focusing on what they can't do that they miss the point. The answers of course can offer clues as to how your next proposal might be positioned.

You can only trade effectively when you understand or gauge the value of an issue in their terms. Part of this you may know from understanding your market, and part may be from any history you may have with the other party. Remember, low cost and high value trade-offs should be worked through as part of your preparations before negotiating begins. Work out the trades. Work out your potential moves.

Remember, generosity engenders greed. Nothing is free in this world and if you start providing unconditional trades, the other party will either get suspicious or just plain greedy.

### *10. Apply analytical skills to manage the value of the deal as the negotiation unfolds*

As a negotiation unfolds, the total value or cost of a deal often becomes more complex as the number of issues increases. This especially includes negotiations which involve a number of interrelated variables; each of which need to be agreed and many which will be interrelated.

Let's say you are agreeing a contract which involves office furniture. There are a range of issues to be agreed. You make a proposal which consists of the shortening of payment terms in return for a lower up-front payment or deposit. In being able to track the progress of your negotiation you need to understand the cost or value of each variable to both you and the other party.

You need to calculate the saving for them if payment is settled over a shorter period of time and how they will value a lower deposit, sometimes literally as the negotiation is unfolding. Of course this goes hand in hand with understanding these values or costs from your own perspective. Using your analytical skills enables you to understand the implications of their response and work out what your next proposal might be:

"We will accept the lower deposit subject to you reducing your payment schedule from your proposed 12 months to 9 months."

How would this affect the total value of the agreement? Should you now park this issue and examine how other terms can be introduced as part of the conversation?

Understanding the implications of trades is critical to working through possibilities and opportunities as we effectively "engineer the deal." That is not to say that you have to be lightning quick with figures or that you have to be highly analytical to work through more complex agreements. You simply have to ensure that through the time you take or the way you delegate or automate (sometimes using spreadsheets) such activities, you are clear about the decisions you are taking.

The less tangible an issue is, the more difficult it can be to value the trade. Some examples might be:

- the changing of opt-out clauses;
- agreement to a testimonial recommendation;
- flexibility in completion dates;
- the offer of exclusivity.

Understanding how to value these types of implications within an agreement is important if you are to trade them effectively. The cost may be little to you and yet hold a significant value to the other party.

During your negotiations track your and their proposals by documenting them, so you can monitor each issue's progress and movement. Track what their last proposal was and what the value of the deal equates to for you. Today, many negotiators use systems or spreadsheets to analyze "what if" scenarios and for tracking proposals, especially when it's an existing contract being renegotiated and the issues under review are consistent.

If, despite this, you struggle with the figures, take your time. Take time out or take someone with you to the negotiation as your "figures person." If you become wrapped up in figures, you will not be in control of the negotiation. If you don't understand the figures, you are in danger of agreeing to something which may prove regrettable.

In the commercial arena, you are negotiating over resources, interests, priorities, preferences, even prejudices. There are a broad range of both tangible and intangible issues, all of which carry a perception of value. Then of course there is money. If you are not aware of the consequences of your proposals, then you are not in control. Make it your business to qualify the worth of all the issues under discussion which you are responsible for negotiating.

### 11. *Create and maintain the appropriate climate for trust*

Creating the appropriate climate for trust is critical if the other party is to accept your ideas as being genuinely helpful and if they are to consider the options you bring to the table. Remember, you are responsible for their feelings and the atmosphere during the negotiation. If they do not feel the ideas being tabled are in the interest of mutual progress they simply will not entertain them.

Where real or perceived conflict of interests exists, trust can be difficult to come by as each party gravitates towards protecting its own interests. The other party may not be as open-minded as you or the balance of power (being in their favor) may mean that they do not need to be so. It takes two to tango. If they want to Hard Bargain, you must be prepared to backtrack and adjust your strategy. Drive at a broader agenda with the aim of building a sustainable agreement rather than engaging in a bruising battle over price.

In a sustainable relationship (9–12 o'clock on the clock face) it is critical to maintain a basis where constructive dialogue can take place without suspicion or the need to compete. Being cooperative, presenting creative proposals and using statements that help progress discussions, rather than antagonizing the other party, requires humility, a broader perspective and an acceptance of the longer-term benefits that a relationship based on trust and respect will bring. Trust takes time to build so patience is needed; yet it can be destroyed in a moment if you cross the other party.

At 4 o'clock on the clock face you are hard bargaining and are without relationship constraints. You can be tough, but when there is a high level of dependency between you, you not only need to be cooperative but should recognize what cooperation provides you with: a basis for creating more value. Your plan to maximize profits remains the same. The way you achieve this is by working with the other party, and changes as you move around to beyond 6 o'clock.

Some companies, in promoting "partnerships", do so as a camouflage as in they need to be regarded as business partners. Their ultimate objective generally remains the same: to maximize profits with or without cooperation depending on how much power they possess.

To gain trust, you have to earn it and this takes time and patience. One way to help achieve this during meetings is by offering information in a controlled and considered manner. The act of sharing information is important to both parties, as it demonstrates that you are prepared to be open and therefore, by implication, to be trusted. Therefore you need to organize and manage what information you are prepared to offer. This is an important part of any negotiator's preparation.

Creating the appropriate climate for trust may require you to do something or be someone you are not. This is where the "conscious negotiator" comes into his or her own. They recognize the egos involved, recognize how the other party wants to be treated and present a cooperative front. They attack the problems and not the people by ensuring the climate in the room remains conducive to building the agreements.

### *12. Develop and use your agenda to help control the negotiation proceedings*

The agenda is effectively a working document for all parties involved that builds the very basis upon which discussions will be held. The agenda helps to shape and control negotiation proceedings. It is there to provide transparency around those variables which will contribute towards the total value of the agreement.

Agreeing on the agenda can often require a negotiation in itself. The issues that feature in your starting agenda will carry a greater emphasis because of the apparent consideration given to them. If formally agreed they will carry more weight and credibility compared with those that are introduced later during discussions.

Further, agreeing on an agenda before the meeting helps ensure that it is "owned" by all involved. If you impose an agenda on the other party, they are more likely to be dismissive and challenging of the issues. You can drive the agenda by building one and providing a draft in advance, asking the other party if they want to add or change anything. Ultimately, both parties agree that all items in need of consideration are listed, and agree that all parties will work from it. This reduces the chances of the other party making last-minute demands that have never been considered. In this scenario, you can then legitimately claim that the new issues were never part of the agreement and that all proposals made to date were offered on the basis that the total set of issues involved were those stated on the agreed agenda. This may not always work as other stakeholders become involved but it can help legitimize your position.

Imagine contracting with a PR firm. Having narrowed down the options to the final two firms, you decide to enter into negotiations to find out where you are most likely to attract the greatest value from. Now, PR at the best of times is a challenging service to measure. However, the basic terms of any agreement will need to feature as part of your agenda. This could include: a retainer fee, notice period, length of contract, range of services, PR training provided, contact requirements and payment terms. Already we have seven issues to be discussed on the agenda and from these there will be further issues relating to performance, compliance and risks linked to each of these seven. The broader the agenda, the more comprehensive your considerations, and the greater scope for shaping the deal and ultimately building a higher value agreement.

### Positioning

Position price, fee or cost about halfway down your agenda. If tackled too early, it can promote unnecessary friction and the risk of premature deadlock. If left to the end, when all of the other issues have been agreed, it could limit room for manoeuvre and drive discussions back around to 4 o'clock.

Some parties choose to outline their entire offer from the outset. Some tendering processes demand your opening position across all variables. Even though you may be in possession of this information you need not be drawn into responding to them all at once. Nothing is agreed until everything is agreed – so issues can be reworked and reshaped – and the shape of the deal may well change many times before your deal is finally agreed. Try to trade off no more than three issues at a time. Any more makes it difficult for them to calculate and, worse still, confusing to understand.

Watch out for hidden agenda points or "red herrings" introduced by the other party with the aim of trading off against them. In doing so, they expect to gain some leverage on issues that are important to them. Where new issues appear on the agenda, set out to qualify their legitimacy. Conversely you may choose to let the other party win some of the lower cost issues and gain the leverage you need to secure those issues that are both important and of high value to you. Remember, if you are going to "lose" or concede on some issues, then trade them conditionally and reluctantly, every time. Make the other party feel that they have had to work hard for the concession. If it is important to them, they will give ground to secure it.

**issue map**

A visual tool for grouping variables and examining the optimum trade-offs. There are many ways of grouping variables together to extract the maximum value. The issue map allows you to "play" with possibilities for formalizing your pre-prepared conditional trades.

From the agenda, an **issue map** (see Chapter 9) can be used to help you visualize and explore options.

Even if you list a draft agenda on a flip chart in the room minutes before your meeting, you have created the illusion that you are prepared. This provides a basis to explore the variables that will need agreeing with the other party in a more collaborative manner.

### *13. Think creatively to develop proposals which help move the deal forward*

Thinking creatively (see Chapter 4, page 118) – that is to say thinking around the issues and possibilities that might not have been considered or traded before – can move the negotiation forwards. Picture yourself as a sculptor: designing, forming, shaping in an artistic manner. Stand back and examine your progress from different angles and perspectives. You are involved in carving out something of much greater value than the sum total of the materials involved. The creative negotiator interprets the possibilities before them and regards the challenge in hand as one of creating value.

If you have a good understanding of the motives and interests of the other party and have been able to gauge the value which they place on issues, especially the less tangible ones, there is potential to introduce proposals which help both of you approach the deal from a different perspective. Creative proposals involve examining the total value opportunity and entertaining discussions and ideas around every issue that will influence the total value. There has to be some degree of trust involved for such discussions to be had, as well as a relative balance in power, otherwise they are likely to drag you back around to hard bargaining at 4 o'clock. However, with all things being equal, the opportunity to build value is served well through creative thinking.

#### The broader the agenda the greater the possibilities and risks

I know of one deal that started with six variables. By the time the first planning session had been completed, we had identified 57 variables, all of which had some bearing on the agreement. We went on to call it the Heinz deal (known for the number of canned and bottled foods it offered for sale) although the deal had nothing to do with canned foods. Every offer was conditional and so we tabled conditional ideas as part of the discussions.

Sometimes you just have to tell the other party what is important; otherwise you are not providing them with the opportunity to make things possible. Detailed exploratory discussions can offer tremendous opportunities to build agendas, which reflect every part of the deal including the risks, performance, compliance, quality, opportunity, communication and many other important components of the relationship.

The ability to remain open-minded and use creative thinking during negotiation is difficult for many people. It is competitiveness, pride, a need to maintain face and ego which prevent many from being open. This results in a dogmatic approach aimed at minimizing risk and "winning."

In negotiation the free and easy thinking patterns associated with creativity are at direct odds with those experienced during moments of perceived conflict. Where conflict exists, we are more inclined to batten down the hatches and are more likely to focus on protecting our position. Absolute possibility, at the other extreme, allows us to explore and be creative rather than being bound by insecurity.

### Creativity in presentation

In reality, however, suspicion can temper open thinking. There is a fine balance between genuinely looking for creative options and protecting your interests. Imagine working with a jigsaw. You have many pieces, which all look similar, but only one will fit into the next hole. Sometimes, finding that piece takes time and patience. It's not much bigger or smaller than the next piece, but when you have found it and present it to the jigsaw, it is accepted.

### *14. Explore options to help gain agreement*

Remove the thought of NO, CAN'T or WON'T and convert this into HOW, no matter how frustrating this might feel at first. Try to resist the temptation to say no. The challenges and frustrations presented in negotiations are there to test us. Deadlock is an option but only after every possible option has been exhausted. This obligation is not only on you but also on the other party. Where peace talks can take years, merger and acquisition negotiations months, the work involved in searching for common areas where agreement can be struck comes from the persistence of those involved. There has to be a belief that there is a solution to be found. The trait of tenacity (page 107, Chapter 4) helps the Complete Skilled Negotiator to explore options continuously, keep the agreement and relationships on track and deliver the possible deal from what once seemed, at best, unlikely.

Making use of the planning tools (see Chapter 9) can help you to visualize possible relationships between the issues. If you can see the whole picture, and the possible links that can be made, this will help you to bring in possibilities which explore options that may not have been considered before.

Take the time to explore options, and continuously consider the deal from their perspective. This is easier said than done, mainly because it requires "positive energy" rather than "defensive energy." Although it's appropriate to remain on your guard, if you are able to park your suspicion and search for alternatives and other options, you will surprise yourself just how many times a last minute solution can be found.

## CONCLUSION

The fourteen behaviors of the Complete Skilled Negotiator underpin effective negotiation performance, regardless of your position on the clock face. With so many ways to negotiate driven by the balance of power, personal traits that encourage individuals to gravitate towards particular skills or negotiate in their preferred manner, is it any wonder that many find it challenging to perform well in all situations?

The key here is to work on developing your capabilities through greater awareness of those skills that you *are* using and to note their effect during your negotiations. Your awareness of how different behaviors will impact on your performance is the first step toward becoming the Complete Skilled Negotiator.

Every business is different and each and every negotiation situation is unique. The value of issues will nearly always be different to both parties and will nearly always be different over time. The personalities involved and relationship dynamics will differ and even those that you understand will change over time. It's with this in mind that the Complete Skilled Negotiator has to be flexible enough to perform in all situations. You cannot consistently perform well if you attempt to employ one "preferred style" for all negotiations. The clock face helps to differentiate this whilst the behaviors help highlight those things that we must do well, depending on the opportunity in hand.

# CHAPTER 6

# The "E" Factor

## THE EFFECT OF HUMAN EMOTION ON NEGOTIATION

"How difficult can negotiation be, it's not rocket science?" No, it is not. I would argue that it is more complex because it involves the most unpredictable of entities: human beings. Emotion makes negotiation highly unpredictable. The impact that this has on the dynamics found in negotiation is what I've defined as the "E" factor.

Negotiators who are less self-aware may struggle to control their emotions and, as a result, become readable and transparent to other negotiators. The more balanced, clearer thinkers use the "E" factor to their advantage like seasoned poker players. The Complete Skilled Negotiator develops an eye for watching your every action and reaction as they gauge what is really going on in your head. Experienced negotiators are:

- conscious of what they are looking for;
- calm in their thought process;
- aware of the sensitivities in play; and
- send you the messages they *want* you to read.

Because every action attracts a reaction, trained negotiators work as hard at calculating how you will react to certain actions, and which signal to send that will most likely influence you during your negotiations.

No matter how many tactics, strategies or variables are in play, it is people who make the decisions and it is people you need to understand; in particular, how they and you behave in the heat of the moment. Unlike an engine, which is mechanically predictable and responds each and every time to the push of a throttle, negotiation and, importantly, people can be unpredictable.

Negotiation requires an attitude of mind based on self-discipline and self-control of emotion. What makes good negotiators into Complete Skilled Negotiators is that they execute negotiations using skills, tactics and strategies but also recognize that attitudes and emotion, hidden or otherwise, will play a part in shaping the outcomes. It is emotional control that allows for clear decision making. Behavioral, mental control and emotional detachment are all needed to get inside the other party's head. Human nature can be foreseeable to some extent but we can never assume the reaction we are going to attract when tabling a proposal, especially when it's not one they are expecting. So the "E" in "E" factor is, you guessed it, for *emotion*. It is a conscious state that allows you to manage, use, manipulate, understand and control it.

Many negotiation decisions in business are still emotionally influenced, even during sizeable complex deals. I'm not suggesting that deals take place without careful diligence or clear criteria and analysis. What I am suggesting from observation is that during negotiations, proposals and considerations are not always considered in the objective manner you might expect. Emotion and ego, as well as enterprise, have a significant role in how decisions are taken.

### *The role of emotion*

Emotion has its place when used in a considered and controlled manner:

- when the risks have been considered (walk out, deadlock, insult);
- when its purpose is to attract a desired reaction; and
- when the seriousness of the issue needs conveying and you are confident that you will not ruin the chances of progress.

There is nothing wrong with a display of emotion during a negotiation, provided it is designed for effect and premeditated. The outburst in the middle of the meeting with a threat to walk away from the deal may appear irrational and hot-headed, but if the action were premeditated and the drama designed to attract a back-down from the other party, the emotional display can serve a useful purpose. This level of risk needs, however, to be a thought-through decision and one that is designed to attract a calculated response in an orchestrated manner. The real danger arises when we allow our decision making to be dictated by our own emotions and we start to react to their demands without realizing it.

### *Understanding our emotions*

Essentially, the emotion experienced by many in negotiation comes from uncertainty, risk, desire and even fear: emotions that we have lived with for millions of years. But today we experience the types of dangers and risks that trigger these emotions less frequently than our ancestors and, more often than not, in a psychological context rather than in the physical form. As a result, we are less practiced and equipped to cope, meaning that even low levels of uncertainty for many can feel quite uncomfortable. For any emotionally driven negotiator this can lead to inappropriate decision making and sub-optimized deals, which is why an understanding of these emotions is important as part of your make-up as a negotiator.

The emotions of fear, hope, anger, envy and greed resonate in us as strongly today as they ever have. Today there are ever more psychological models available to help us define what drives emotion, how people cope with it and the effect that it will have on you. Yet, when faced with confrontation over a price increase in a negotiation are we any more able to cope with what this does to our thinking and ability to perform? The answer is: only through greater levels of self-awareness.

Negotiation is uncomfortable (see page 6, Chapter 1), and when negotiating on behalf of your business, you are effectively being paid to be uncomfortable. If you concede unnecessarily or capitulate on a deal, you are not delivering on behalf of your employer.

### *The tell-tale signs of stress*

When you prepare for any negotiation, take time to consider the dynamics of the relationship, the stakeholders and the hierarchical levels at which communication needs to take place. It is no surprise just how often personalities play a critical part in the viability of the deal, so much so that the absolute value of the deal can be regarded as secondary to the overall viability of the relationship.

The stress associated with the perception of differentiated and competing positions requires you to maintain total self-control.

This has to come across in the way you state your proposals. This is especially true when you find yourself, even momentarily, feeling as though you are being "unfair." The process you are involved in should not be driven by fairness, yet the personal values which you hold will challenge you and your level of discomfort.

The pressure and stress that you experience in negotiation, however mild, are difficult to suppress and have their way of showing themselves through your physical actions. The stress you experience when tabling or rejecting proposals can start to exhibit itself through your movements. The risk of touching your face, scratching your nose, brushing your hands through your hair, tapping your pen, folding your arms, or tapping your feet when making a proposal are all illustrations of emotion, and will be seen by the other party who will be watching for them. You may not even be aware of it. Most are not. However, the other person will be watching every move you make.

More experienced negotiators learn to adapt to becoming more comfortable with being uncomfortable. This is achieved through heightened levels of self-awareness and becoming experienced in doing what is necessary from an objective standpoint, rather than allowing themselves to be victims of their emotion.

If you witness negotiators exhibiting these fidgety types of behaviors it may well mean nothing, other than an adjustment of their position. Body language, and its meanings, tends only to be relevant when change, speed or the timing of movement correlates with something that has happened. If the other party responds to your proposal immediately, insisting that they will not or cannot accept the offer, watch for how they are behaving physically as they respond. It is likely there will be some emotion involved. It is possible they mean it and it is also possible that they don't. Look for a correlation in body language or facial expressions if there is more than one of them negotiating. The change in behavior that is taking place means that the other party is involved in protecting their position. This is usually most recognizable when they are stating a position, rejecting a position or making a point.

- Listen to what they are saying, the way they are saying it and what they do not say.
- Listen to whether they justify what they are saying.
- Listen to whether they go on to sell what they have just said.

The Complete Skilled Negotiator will see, hear, read and interpret the meaning behind this as part of getting inside the other party's head.

You may possess the nerve which allows you to control your emotions when challenged by pressure. The pressures you face will usually be driven by your current circumstances and perhaps the fear of concluding a bad deal or no deal at all. The more options you have, for example, (behavior 14, page 163, Chapter 5) the less dependency, the lower the immediate pressure and the less the need to cope with the potential of high emotion during your meeting. You may feel you are capable of holding your nerve (remember trait 1, Chapter 4, page 105) and that your mindset is balanced when it comes to managing the emotions and stresses of negotiating, but it is amazing how a sudden change in circumstances can shake the steady ground you thought you were standing on.

If you, or those who negotiate on your behalf, experience high levels of anxiety (often found in personal negotiations), the resulting agreements are more likely to be compromised. The stress and anxiety of the process can lead you to concede or conclude agreements too early. Negotiating effectively requires nerve, as well as a mindset which recognizes that it is not personal, it is business. Negotiators I have worked with who appear at least to have high levels of emotional control will mentally separate the people they negotiate with from the business of working on the deal. Whether you empathize with them or not is immaterial: it's about the quality of the agreement and the quality of the outcome of your negotiating efforts. Yes, of course it is helpful if they like you but this is not your objective. Work on being liked if you believe it will lead to greater levels of trust and more scope for building value, but not on being liked simply because "that's the sort of person I am and it's how I prefer to work."

### Negotiation colleague to colleague

The same skills apply for internal negotiations as they do for external, commercially based negotiations. However, internal negotiations require us to manage relationships even more carefully and work towards solutions in a constructive, mature and sustainable way. The clashing of two department heads over resources, budgets or project timescales can still lead to emotionally fuelled encounters. Such discussions can frequently spiral out of control as two hot-headed managers become consumed by the underlying inter-departmental rivalries and become unable to focus on resolving the specific issue at hand in the best interests of the company. The principle of negotiating inside your own business with others, mapping out the issues and examining all the options is no different from negotiations held with customers or suppliers. However, where emotions start to influence discussions, objectivity is challenged which can make agreements far more difficult to reach.

## CONSCIOUS COMPETENT

An unconscious incompetent negotiator is one that is not aware of the impact of their actions and therefore generally suboptimizes the agreements they complete. This consciousness state also results in denial of the relevance or usefulness of even needing to develop negotiation skills. Any negotiator must become conscious of their own incompetences before the development of the new skills or learning can begin. The key to becoming more effective as a negotiator is to become a "conscious competent," by being able consciously to perform the skill or ability. As you become aware of the existence and relevance of the specific negotiation skills and the effect they have on output you will also grow a greater awareness of your own shortcomings. The negotiator achieves "conscious competence" when they can perform at will. They need to concentrate and think in order to perform the skill; the skill is not yet "second nature" or "automatic" and requires the negotiator to operate as a "conscious competent." Over time the skills become so practiced that they enter the unconscious parts of the brain and become "second nature." Common examples of unconscious competence are driving, sports activities, typing, manual dexterity tasks, listening and communicating.

However, this advanced state of consciousness too has its own handicap in that it can encourage you to assume too much based on previous experience. So remaining in the "conscious competent" state for the purpose of negotiating is highly appropriate.

If you have ever negotiated with children and been on the receiving end of their demands, you will know how emotional blackmail, outbursts and intransigence can be very powerful, irrespective of whether you can accommodate their demands or not.

**CASE STUDY**

At the age of three, my son Andrew came to me asking for an ice cream, to which I replied: "You can't have an ice cream now, your dinner will be served in ten minutes, you can have one later." "But I want an ice cream now daddy," he said. I reminded him again that he could have an ice cream later; feeling that I had put my rational case forward and that would be the end. My son's response to this however was to scream: "That's not fair, I want one now, not later; give me one now, I want one now," and the tears started to flow. By this point, I was starting to feel bad and replied, "OK, just the one but don't tell your mother." I was clearly inside my own head. His emotional outburst had worked on me and he got his result. My response of course had set a precedent, as I had rewarded the very behavior I should have sought to prevent, just for some peace. Needless to say, it wasn't a great example of parenting and my future negotiation tactics with my kids were rather more considered.

### *Becoming a consciously competent negotiator through understanding TA*

Back in the 1950s Dr Eric Berne defined the ego states known to us today as transactional analysis (TA). In the book *I'm OK, You're*

*OK*, the author Thomas Harris analyzed Berne's work which was made up of definitions of ego states and how they affect the way we communicate with each other. These are defined as the roles of:

- Parent (critical and nurturing)
- Adult
- Child (free and adaptive).

These are communication styles that we all use subconsciously whilst communicating with others. They are used to varying degrees dependent on the relationships in play. Importantly, within negotiation, these ego states resonate in the language and behavior used which can directly impact on expectations, respect, irrationality, arrogance and other attitudes exercised during discussions.

TA also provides insights that help to explain how we are programmed to communicate and how we relate to others in negotiation, as well as the way we think, feel and behave.

### The "critical parent" ego state

Through our lives and over time we conform to society, adopting the attitudes and behaviors of those around us. We even adopt the values, beliefs and use the same verbal statements as used by our parents. The language of the critical parent's ego state, is "black and white," "right and wrong" or "good and bad," with very few shades of grey. "You always get it wrong," "you never make it on time," and "you don't understand what I am saying," suggesting that they are right, you are wrong, and that they are in a position to judge. They make the rules, judge and criticize others. You might view this as short-sighted or even arrogant. However, what is important in your negotiations is that you do not allow such communication to affect the way you read the situation. This ego state can relate to anyone. Listen to any group of children talking and you will hear one member of the group talking as if they were in charge, especially when playing games.

Later in life, this type of "critical parent" language is typically used by autocrats. It is associated with ignorance or arrogance as it implies that the individual has only one view and is not open to alternatives. Their direct communication will involve them telling you what you will do and what you won't do, what you can do and what you can't do; as if to suggest that they can control such demands. In negotiation, some people have been known to use this stance to take control. The power in the language used by "critical parents" can be a difficult force to reason with when they remain inflexible and stubborn, especially when they are negotiating from a position of power. They will know it and will use it, sometimes naturally and sometimes orchestrated but always aimed at controlling your aspirations. The result is that those on the receiving end of the discussion are at risk of conforming to the situation and adopting the opposite ego state of the "child," leaving them vulnerable to accepting a sub-optimal deal.

### The "nurturing parent" ego state

Parents are, however, also nurturing and Berne explains how this natural state not only exists in people who exhibit parental ego states but can be manipulated by those communicating as a "child." The "nurturing parent" wants to advise and guide. They want respect and want to be needed. They want to protect, so any "child" showing respect and asking for help is likely to attract a positive response from a nurturing parent.

#### The "child" ego state

The "child" ego state is also made up of two ego states: the "free child" and the "adapted child."

The "free child" is spontaneous, creative, fun loving in their attitude and communication whereas the adapted child is rebellious, non-compliant and manipulative.

These behaviors, thoughts and feelings are replayed from our own childhood and, depending on our circumstances, will feature in how we communicate throughout our lives. This can result in our feeling victimized by the rules that others lay down, or underpin our desire to challenge authority.

Ingrained in our memories are the emotions we experienced as children: "It's not fair," "It's not my fault," "See what you've made me do." The "child" commonly shirks responsibility, is sometimes manipulative, sometimes subservient, but is always a product of those around them. "Please, please, please ...," "I want it now." Children, not to be confused with the "child" ego state, can be very adult-like when playing with their peers, but in the company of adults they behave in a quite different way.

### *Responses to ego states*

In negotiation, behaving in the "parent" ego state can result in others adopting the behavioral response of a "child" ego state. Where you find yourself negotiating with a "critical parent" character, who happens to be holding a position of power within the negotiation, rather than simply arguing against them as an opposing parent, you may choose to appeal to their nurturing parent instinct. Two "parents" clashing is simply two egos vying for control and domination which will frequently lead to impasse, and the breakdown of the relationship and any pending negotiations.

If you adopt the "child" ego state, you are of course effectively manipulating their ego by asking them how they might be able to help you, given your weaker position. There are risks to this, in that they may choose to manipulate the situation even further. However, once the "parent" recognizes that there is no fight to be had, and that you are asking for help, their nurturing ego is triggered and they generally become far more accommodating.

### The "adult" ego state

When in our "adult" ego state, we are more able to see people and situations as they are, rather than being intimidated or manipulative. This state allows us to manage the person, people or situation we are confronted with far more objectively. We draw on our past experiences and use them in the present to weigh and consider the options. We are more likely to make decisions based on a pragmatic, objective analysis of any given situation, rather than be swayed by the emotional ego that exists in the "child" or "parent" states. If there was a preferred default position from which to negotiate, it would be the "adult" ego state.

Listen and watch out for the behavior of the "black and white," "right and wrong" dominant "parent."

Listen and watch out for the positioning of the "child," who seeks to seduce you, or make irrational demands, in that they need your help and appeal to your sense of parenting.

The "adult" on the other hand is objective in thought, can accommodate many shades of grey, recognize irrational behavior and sees most types of behavior and language for what they are. They generally operate as conscious competent negotiators.

Clearly though, this is only an ego state and even "adults" are still susceptible to the way others communicate with them and can still be influenced into adopting other ego states during negotiations. Imagine you were challenged on your opening position by a "parent", who tells you how ridiculous you are being, and not to come back until you are prepared to be sensible. The decision here is whether to respond as a "critical parent" and challenge, with the risk of intensifying the conflict, or adopt the ego state of the "free child" and ask them for help; for example, in how you can make the proposal more mutually acceptable, attracting a more sympathetic response. If you are not sure, and really cannot do with playing ego games with the other party, you may choose to maintain your composure as an "adult," dismiss their behavior, and wait patiently for them to calm down before continuing. As always, it depends on the circumstances. What is important is that we recognize these states in others as well as ourselves and that we adapt accordingly, rather than continue, oblivious to the emotion influencing the dynamics of the relationship and communication.

The "E" factor can make or break a deal, or the longer-term prospects of a relationship. This makes self-awareness an important part of the Complete Skilled Negotiator's make-up. Those who are successful at negotiating in the long term are more likely to have "adult-to-adult" relationships, although in "the real world," irrational behavior for whatever reason is in no short supply.

## YOUR VALUES

Your personal values and your business values are often very similar. They can be based on such qualities as integrity, honesty, reliability and others. They provide you with the parameters to judge what you believe is fair, what behavior you find acceptable and the degree to which you are prepared to allow others to use the power they have during your dealings.

Your values may well provide you with balance in how you lead your life, how you make decisions, interpret right from wrong, and so on. However, in negotiation, they can often serve to distort your thinking (see page 128 on clear thinking). Whether the behavior of the other party is ethical, "fair" or "right" is of little consequence in negotiation. If they have the power and decide to be irrational with it, it is your job to manage the situation as you find it. It is not the time to start making value judgements. Cling to your ideals and you will become emotionally challenged and compromised.

Getting upset or angry about the "unfair" or "disproportionate" terms the other party is demanding is unlikely to attract any sympathy or empathy, let alone a better result. In fact, it will probably promote the opposite as you are likely to appear needy or emotional and will lose respect.

## EMOTIONAL INTELLIGENCE

If there is one critical competency central to effective negotiation, I would suggest it is "emotional intelligence." It underpins the balance of communication between you and those you negotiate with, and promotes the concept of negotiating from inside their head.

In his 1995 book, *Emotional Intelligence,* Daniel Goleman describes how emotional intelligence is made up of two parts. He claims that to be effective in business, you need to have a high level of self-awareness and self-control around your emotions and those of the other party.

- Firstly, by understanding yourself, your intentions, your responses and your own behavior.
- Secondly, by understanding others and their feelings.

This is critical in negotiations because you are responsible for the feelings of those you negotiate with. Antagonize the other party and watch any hope of cooperation dissolve. Goleman goes on to describe the five "domains" of emotional intelligence:

1. Knowing our emotions.
2. Managing your own emotions.
3. Motivating yourself.
4. Recognizing and understanding other people's emotions.
5. Managing relationships and the emotions of others.

Extroverts, who tend to be more communicative, tend to be more openly emotional people. They are more inclined to share and articulate their views, likes and dislikes. However, extroverts are faced with a greater challenge because the control required during a negotiation involves a greater level of self-discipline than it does with introverts, who are naturally more considered in their responses.

Introverts are more inclined to reflect, weigh and consider before responding.

Imagine watching a film which involves two parties negotiating. The actors are engaged in a negotiation, and one of them is performing so poorly that it starts to make you cringe. "Why did they say that?", "You've just given away your position by saying that," "I would never have responded in that way," you think to yourself.

During negotiation workshops at The Gap Partnership, we often provide challenging case study exercises for individuals and groups to negotiate with each other. The negotiations are recorded on video to help the attendees observe and learn about the appropriateness of their behavior given their objectives. We help them to analyze their planning, behavior, self-control and performance. Today we work with hundreds of case studies from our library, which are each designed to focus on different learning outcomes in different industries, working with different groups of negotiating variables. There are some multi-issue case studies which so accurately lead to predictable behavior that I have used them time after time. You could predict minutes before an attendee negotiating did something, what they were going to do. The coaching that follows is based around the appropriateness of their motives, emotions and decision making, which provides a powerful lesson in self-awareness every time.

But what was it that made their actions so predictable? Competitiveness? Pride? The need to perform? A desire to use the skills we had already covered to positive effect? It was their ego and the competitive case-study situation that led to a narrowing of the mind, resulting in a dismissal of the need for humility and for any consideration of the broader issues. It becomes personal, despite the considerable commercial experience and background of those I have worked with. It drove individuals (thousands of them over the years) to justify their often short-term irrational behavior because of the pressure they felt resulting from the circumstances they had been placed in. They were willing, under certain circumstances, to compete, even though their brief was to focus on the total value opportunity.

Negotiating agreements successfully in business can be very challenging in that commercial pressures combined with an obligation to deliver will naturally stimulate your competitiveness. Business is all about "winning" and outperforming your competitors. However, your competitor is not the person you are negotiating with. From the many organizations where I have spent time facilitating negotiations, I have concluded that the bigger the desire to "win," the greater the chance of distorted thinking during negotiations and the less emotional intelligence is used. Resist the temptation to allow your ego to color your judgement. Winning in negotiation means building successful agreements which the other party will deliver against. It is about building value and enhancing the bottom line. In some cases it might be about gaining a commitment to change that minimizes disruption, or simply reducing the risks associated with an existing arrangement. What it is not about is you, or whether you have won. If you allow this thought or feeling to dominate your motivation your performance will most likely be compromised.

## THE ART OF LOSING

Negotiation is about the art of losing, or the art of letting others have *your* way. With your ego out of the way, and your attitude firmly focused on the outcome of the agreement, you are free to behave in any way you believe to be appropriate to your interests. Being what you need to be and doing what you need to do includes allowing the other party to enjoy the "symbols of success" whilst you focus on the total value of the agreement. This means understanding others and their needs and then trading off no more than you need to in order to optimize your net position. It means letting them win on items of less significance whilst you focus on the more significant, value-adding variables. You could argue that you cannot afford to set precedents by allowing them to win the psychological battle even on some issues (depending on whether there is an ongoing trading relationship or not), or that if you concede on certain issues they will expect this in the future. However, your job as a negotiator is also to help the other party to feel as though they have won.

### CASE STUDY

Imagine a new customer or supplier with whom you have built an understanding over a number of meetings. You have invested time working through the specification of the deal, agreed on how your relationship will work, agreed the service agreement and a continuous improvement programme. They have had your proposal for some time, so they are clearly aware of your fee structure, which has not been challenged to date. You feel the deal is moving in the right direction and report back to your boss to this effect.

They suddenly introduce a further stage to the process that involves you having to meet and agree terms with a different function. With no notice or prior mention the procurement department suddenly demand to be involved in agreeing the terms.

Procurement departments are mostly uninterested in the investment you have made or many of the value-added specifications which you have already introduced during your discussions. They are generally charged with simply getting the best price for the business. This may not be universal across all organizations but I have observed this in many of the 100-plus corporations that I have worked with. They start with your price list and demand a high discount rate, poor payment terms whilst ignoring other conditions. Typically you are also given set timescales around the decision-making process, after which they enter a period of "denied access," a tactic where they are suddenly unavailable for whatever reason. They have effectively taken control. The relationship that initially seemed to exist at 10 o'clock has moved to 4 o'clock and you are now Hard Bargaining. You were not prepared for this because you thought that at 10 o'clock, you would be building an agenda based on value creation with your customer. You try to contact your sponsor but they now seem to be unavailable.

Sound familiar?

In situations like this when you feel as though you are losing control of the relationship, emotions can take over and your decision-making capacity can become compromised. Your position and scope to negotiate also become compromised by circumstances and the proactivity being employed by your prospective customer. Your immediate reaction may be, "this is not fair, not right and I'm not even sure I want to work with them anymore," which runs counter to your business interests. Despite your reactive stance, now is the time to consider your response and advise them of your position. Develop your strategy and do not react emotionally. There are two options for preventing this type of situation *before you even start to negotiate*.

1 Always establish whether there is a buying process involved that you should be aware of.
2 Always identify the decision maker(s) and any other stakeholders who are involved in the sign-off of agreements.

## MANAGING THE EMOTIONAL NEED FOR SATISFACTION

We touched briefly on the need for satisfaction in Chapter 1 (page 8). The need that individuals have for "satisfaction" – meaning getting a better deal than what was originally available – is so strong that many negotiators use relative positioning and inflexibility at the start of a negotiation with the aim of letting the other party achieve what they thought at the beginning of discussions to be difficult if not impossible. Open your tough negotiations at a position you know they will reject and it is the start of the process of "give and take," which will allow you to start managing the other party's need for satisfaction. Many inexperienced negotiators start with a figure that they know the other party can accept because of the fear of hearing the word "no."

Get used to the word "no." When you open with a position which is extreme and yet realistic, you are going to hear it a lot. It is part of the process and you should expect it. Keep the dialogue open and they are less likely to walk away. If they tell you they can't or won't agree to your opening offer, invite them to tell you how close they can get to your offer. It keeps the dialogue going and it gets them to talk about your position. Rather than allowing them to get emotional, ask them what they would agree to rather than what they will not agree to. Then stop and consider your next move.

One of the benefits of opening first in negotiation is that you create an anchor, a position to move from and a position for them to attack. This should be on the right side of where you expect to finish up, rather than reacting to their position and playing in their "ball park." Be proactive and open first. Take the rejection and then move forward. You are managing their satisfaction and at the same time involved in the process of securing the best possible deal. It provides you with the opportunity to maximize the deal whilst still allowing them to take emotional satisfaction from finishing on their own break point.

### CASE STUDY

Imagine, as an account manager, you have been authorized to offer your buyer an investment payment of $200,000 to support the promotion of your product. The buyer is aiming to attract a figure of $250,000. You are able to offer the investment, subject to conditions that will help promote your products, which needs to realize a long-term benefit many times the $200,000. You open discussions with the agenda covering all the conditions and a $125,000 investment offer to your buyer. Over several meetings, you manage to secure all of your requirements in return for $180,000. Given your starting position, the buyer feels that you worked hard and have offered concessions to get to the final figure of $180,000, and improved their position to a point that they feel satisfied.

You might have offered the full $200,000, but why use it just because it has been made available? You are satisfied that the concessions you have received in return are good value and believe that the contract has every chance of success. In other words, their satisfaction and commitment to the deal will come from the motivation of securing a deal which was hard earned and therefore worth having. The harder you work on a deal, the more challenging it is to complete, and so the commitments are more likely to be honored.

Banks and real-estate agents are known for trying to manage satisfaction, but often the individuals responsible for the negotiations simply don't have the nerve to carry through the transaction in a controlled manner. The estate agent who tells you: "our fee is 1.75% of the selling price, but we know it's a competitive market ... so we are prepared to do it for 1.5%." Did I get any satisfaction from this move? No. It was quick, unconditional and transparent. They didn't even wait for a response, or find out whether I have already been offered 1.5% elsewhere, or establish that I wanted to work with them anyway because of their great service levels for example. The bank manager who states: "we are currently offering our business clients an overdraft facility of base plus 4%. However, in your case we are prepared to offer base plus 3.5%."

Why? So that I feel better? I did not have to work for it or even meet a condition. It wasn't even a deciding factor at the time, so why offer it? Satisfaction comes from having to work for it. Even those in the crowds at the sales have to hunt down the deals in the high street, investing hours of time to get the 25% off deal. They may not have negotiated, but they have invested their time and effort. To those involved in the process, they will feel satisfied with their bargain.

If someone agrees too easily, you have a decision and commitment which can just as easily be reversed. Psychologically, things that are hard to attain carry a greater value. Deals that have been hard fought for are more likely to be honored. Regard the process of working towards agreement as an investment in the agreement's sustainability or likelihood of it being honored.

Remember that you can get a great price but a lousy deal if the other party do not deliver on their commitments as has been agreed. For example, if it does not arrive on time, or if it doesn't do the job you need it for – the price makes up only one part of the overall equation.

Working within fixed budgets can mean that your budget is finite. When restricted in this way, it is important to understand the effect this may have on what you agree regarding specification. Will the product or service be de-specified to allow for the price? Is this clear up-front or is it likely to come to light only once the agreement has been made? Maintaining focus and discipline throughout your negotiation means ensuring you are thorough when it comes to covering all the issues, risks, specification, timing and any other factors which could result in you receiving less than what you believe you had agreed to. Unfortunately, those who remain in denial use budget constraints as an excuse for poor deals that often fail to deliver.

## TRUST, TACTICS AND EMOTIONS

The trust and respect that you build in your relationships allow for discussion and the opportunity to build agreements. Your energy can then be spent on the deal rather than on positioning and managing the emotional needs of those involved. Between 9 o'clock and 12 o'clock this relationship state provides the ideal place to maximize value. However, where tactics are used and become obvious, trust dilutes, the negotiation becomes more positional and decisions become more emotionally driven and possibilities deteriorate.

Some negotiators say they want to work in a partnership and yet behave tactically back around at 6 o'clock. They may even start to introduce demands that they don't even want. Why? Because they are attempting to provide you with the satisfaction of negotiating the demands off the table and "winning." The issues "to be lost" are usually built into the agenda to provide them with credibility.

I have seen the red herring used and work on many occasions. However, like most tactics, it can be transparent and they can prove detrimental to your interests, especially if you need to maintain trust and integrity for the relationship to work. It can also result in the discussions being emotionally charged and most likely result in deals providing less value.

## CASE STUDY

An IT outsourcing consultancy, Data Search, introduced an agenda featuring 21 items.

Three of the items tabled seemed out of line with the priorities that had been established in earlier meetings. The three items were made up of an extensive notice period, an option to move their support centre out of the country, and annual price increases equating to 2% above inflation. This was on a potential five-year deal. The annual price increase demand was inconsistent with how they worked with other organizations. The buyers knew this because they had done their research. The investment that Data Search were making could not possibly justify a twelve-month notice period and one of the reasons they had been selected in the first place was because of their UK operation … and they knew it. Rather than getting into arguments involving these three issues, the meeting was adjourned. Emotions were running high and there was a real danger of contract discussions breaking down. The agenda was rewritten and presented as a condition of continued discussions. The effect was a dilution in trust and greater tensions between the two parties. The effect on Data Search was the realization that not only were the buyers prepared, but that they were now going to have to work hard to make headway on any of the remaining issues.

## VISIBLE EMOTION

Visible emotion is also used tactically in negotiation. One such tactic known as the "Professional Flinch" (page 139, Chapter 5), which I have covered in more detail in Chapter 8, involves one party making their opening proposal and the other reacting with an exaggerated emotional reaction, implying that the offer is ridiculous. The emotion, orchestrated, is designed to provide a far more powerful form of rejection than a simple "no." As a negotiator you need to read the situation and be confident of your actions. There is no place for uncontrolled emotion in negotiation. As a Complete Skilled Negotiator, you need to be in control of your thinking, reactions, what you say and what you decide not to say.

Another way of deliberately controlling visible emotions is when negotiators make power statements during the opening exchanges of a discussion as part of anchoring the aspirations of the other party. As they do so, they are consciously waiting for the reactions to gauge how far they might push a particular issue. For example: "We're pleased we've been able to get together to discuss some of the issues around our compensation claim today," or "Clearly you recognize that this is most unusual and that any settlement is likely to take months if not years to conclude given the complexity of the issue." The anchor statement may have no substance at all. The person making the statement is watching and listening for the emotional signals that suggest rejection or acceptance of the statement. The Complete Skilled Negotiator would counter with an alternative statement. This effectively reverses the power statement back to the other party.

Emotion, pressure and stress are commonplace in negotiation, if you know where to look. With the implications of deadlock, the responsibility to deliver, and the frustration which can come with working through agreements, self-control often gives way to our subconscious. You start to do things you are not even aware of. Most people I have worked with do not believe this until they see it for themselves on video, but non-verbal communication becomes exaggerated during stressful times, especially when statements or threats are being made.

Telling the other party what you *will* do at any given point in your discussions (even if it's not the best offer you could make) is a useful discipline for getting them to focus on your position. You have to accommodate patience and frustration whilst options are considered. Sometimes the other party themselves may start to show signs of emotion or stress. Usually this is most evident when responding to or making a proposal.

Imagine you know that you can agree at $1000, but have opened your position at $600. They ask you: "is that your best price?", to which you reply, "that's the price I am prepared to pay." They then make you an offer of $1100. You say: "I can move to $725 but that will need to include the service agreement and delivery by Monday." All the time you are seeking to trade price against other value items but, in the back of your mind, you know that you can go further and would be prepared to do so if the alternative was to lose the deal, which even at $1000 is as good as your best alternative. They pause, having heard you say $725, and there is a moment of silence. Are they thinking about it, preparing to walk away or considering their next move? The 20 seconds that have passed feel like 5 minutes.

Their silence may be suggesting to you that your offer is ridiculous and that they have no interest in further conversations. The fact that they are still in discussions is a non-verbal suggestion that there is some level of interest. The Complete Skilled Negotiator understands that nothing happens by accident in negotiation. Everything, every movement, statement, response and moment of silence happens for a reason, so will maintain composure, watch, and listen.

Your job as a negotiator is to read and interpret the correlation between what is being *said* and *how* the other party is *behaving*.

During the experiential negotiation workshops I have provided the opportunity to negotiate agreements whilst being recorded on video, allowing for detailed analysis of everything which takes place. It allows negotiators to see for themselves the degree to which their actions and emotions are visible. Most people completely deny that they would give any type of signal away until they see themselves on camera. Once they have and accept this, it results in a significant leap in consciously controlled performances. Listen to what they say, watch what they do and then calculate your response.

Conscious negotiators are capable of active listening. This involves intentionally demonstrating to others that you are listening, engaged and open-minded, if that's what you want them to think. In other words, they are skilled at providing the signals through their own body language that they want the other party to receive. Part of getting into the other party's head is getting them to think what you *want* them to think.

### *Emotional ego*

How many times have you seen emotion or ego-fuelled behavior at charity auctions, let alone business auctions? The entire event is geared to provide maximum personal exposure in the room. The compère walks around calling the bidders by their name: "now that's $5000 for the football shirt, has Mr John Smith the nerve to increase his bid?" As he turns to Mr Smith, so does the attention of the audience. Of course Mr Smith has the nerve, and he doesn't want to lose face. These businessmen at the auctions who are clearly successful, and who have probably worked very hard for such sums, regard this as a fun process. They are seduced by the immediate public recognition for their generosity and dismiss the very judgement they usually exercise that probably helped them make the money in the first place. It's for charity. It is their money (although not always) so I can understand their "fun." However, on many occasions similar actions have been witnessed in the business world where the egos of those involved use "company money," fuelled by the need to win, and exercise disregard for the very shareholders they are working on behalf of.

Emotion erodes objectivity. If your spouse was being held captive and a ransom was being demanded for their release, the last person who should negotiate the agreement is you. You are emotionally involved and therefore immediately compromised. You would probably give everything you own for their release, probably in your first offer, assuming the kidnappers had not already stated their demand. You should of course delegate the role of negotiating to another person. They may be no more competent than you at negotiating, but they will be without the emotional attachment that you have to the outcome.

## CASE STUDY

Tony experienced the frustrations of negotiating whilst managing emotion first-hand. His wife, Sue, fell in love with a house. They went to view it three times over a two-week period before deciding to place their own house on the market and make an offer on their dream home at below the asking price. Sue had spent two weeks visualizing how she wanted to decorate the house, how the old barn situated close to the house could be renovated and what furniture she would place where. They even went to the local pub as part of their "checking out the village" research. The property was on the market for £510,000. Their original offer of £450,000 was rejected and a counter offer was made by the seller of £490,000, leaving them with a £40,000 difference in position. They needed to hold their nerve and bring in other variables. They knew that employing the gardener who had worked for ten hours a week for the past 15 years was an important consideration for the seller. Sue wanted to explore every way possible to bridge the gap: "Let's just borrow more, we can afford it," and securing the house became the only thing of importance in her mind.

In her mind the consequences of borrowing more thus became unimportant relative to the seller saying yes. Within a day, the seller had received an offer from a competing would-be buyer for £500,000. They were now going to have to offer the seller more money than he had said he was prepared to accept only 24 hours earlier if they still wanted this house. And Sue wanted this house. They decided to match the price of the other bid at £500,000 after qualifying that it was a genuine bid by someone in a comparable position to them. Now Tony had the market (supply and demand) and emotion to contend with and no suitable alternative (BATNA) available to him. Having ignored some basic preparation principles, he was now involved in a bidding process with his wife Sue by his side. At least he had set a break point (the original asking price of £510,000) which they had both agreed they would not exceed. This was just as well because they eventually reached this, agreed to pay the equivalent of their break point to secure the house. Had they not set their break point they might have paid even more. As it turned out, both parties stopped bidding on the same figure. By the time the bidding had stopped ten days later, Tony and Sue had sold their own house, were ready to proceed and secured the house because of their improved circumstances. The competition had driven the price up, their break point had protected them and the desire and emotion had ensured that they did not walk away. However, had the bidding process not started, things may well have finished differently.

## CONCLUSION

To listen, understand, calculate, think, and respond without emotion takes a tremendous amount of mental capacity. This is what we mean by the "E" factor. It is what differentiates you as a Complete Skilled Negotiator from others because it leads to optimum performance. The gymnast may have many skills in speed, agility and strength, but if they do not have balance, they will never excel. For many this proves a difficult discipline because some attributes do not come naturally, but they can be learnt. If you do, however, find yourself in a difficult position, adjourn the meeting and remove yourself before you become psychologically and financially compromised. If in doubt of what to do next, do nothing, otherwise you will probably regret it. Planning and preparation should help you avoid such situations, but with negotiations taking unpredictable twists and turns, you should never feel obliged to conform and remain in the room. If in doubt, get out. The implications of time and consequence are usually cited as the reasons why people continue in discussions, even when the implications of their position are unclear.

Time and circumstance is the most powerful influencer of value in negotiation. Whether real or perceived, the changes it brings can trigger the emotional reactions of those involved. Time can change everything, including the balance of power between the parties involved. This in turn can quickly impact on the style of negotiation in play, the way relationships work and the degree of integrity or fairness that is in play.

Even where strong dependent relationships exist, i.e. with your boss, your husband, your business partner or your customer, with challenge and change, emotion is never far away. It is the "E" factor that so often differentiates the outcomes of agreements, meaning in negotiation that the predictability of how others will behave can never be assumed.

# CHAPTER 7

# Authority and Empowerment

## UNDERSTANDING EMPOWERMENT

Your negotiations can only progress if communication flows and those who are involved are allowed to take decisions. Therefore, understanding the role of empowerment in your negotiation is fundamental to managing the relationships and communications which stand between you and progress. Furthermore, the more empowered you or they are, the more scope you have with which to negotiate, the more scope to be creative and the more scope to build value in your agreements.

However, with empowerment comes exposure and this brings with it risk. It is this risk that organizations seek to control by empowering individuals with limits, or caps, beyond which they must escalate to higher authority. Too much empowerment and any individual can become dangerous or vulnerable and therefore so can the organization they work for.

The Complete Skilled Negotiator will understand empowerment in terms of:

- how it can be used to protect you;
- how it affects your ability to be creative;
- how it affects your ability to build value;
- how it affects the other party's thinking and behavior.

Essentially, it is the degree to which you can negotiate and take decisions without having to refer or escalate them to a higher authority. In other words, empowerment relates to the scope and range of variables and the authority within which you have to negotiate or operate. If you regard empowerment as simply a gauge to broaden or narrow your trading opportunities, or to provide "stop limits" up to which you can negotiate, you can start to get a feel for how empowerment can work for you, as well as against you.

To negotiate collaboratively on the left-hand side of the clock face (6–12 o'clock) requires the scope or empowerment to work with many variables and possibilities. Limiting this, as many organizations do, can help you to protect yourself from the escalation and disempowerment tactics used by others. So getting this right is fundamental to where you will finish up on the clock face. As with any balancing act, the setting of appropriate limits helps to maximize opportunity, but without overexposure.

## WE ARE ALL EMPOWERED TO SOME DEGREE

Great negotiators tend to be unsung heroes. Great deals become so over time as the contract delivers the value it was intended to offer, rather than necessarily at the time when the deal was completed. Negotiators often work as part of a team which can involve specialist lawyers, finance directors and others. Because the last person to become involved in the negotiation dealings is the boss, the act of negotiation is usually delegated further down the line, further diluting the transparency of who is actually controlling events. And when the deal is done, the need for confidentiality as well as the need to protect the operations of those companies involved means that the true facts and figures agreed are rarely publicized to the degree to which you can measure the relative performance of the negotiators involved.

Most high-profile negotiators tend to be political figures or union leaders, because they use PR as part of posturing during or leading up to discussions. However, these individuals neither work by themselves nor are they fully empowered to negotiate on all issues. Using the press and media is part of how they frame and publicize their position and progress to those they represent, the parties they are negotiating with, and any other third parties.

One of my personal experiences as a negotiator involved facilitating a highly charged negotiation between a Japanese electronics company and a trade union in the UK. The level of trust between the parties involved, together with the climate of the meeting and the relationship was poor, hence the need to bring in a neutral to facilitate events. On my advice to my client, I was provided with no scope with which to negotiate, which allowed me to focus on the process and not be drawn on specific proposals. My role included helping the parties with establishing solutions starting with why they thought they could not agree to the terms which had already been tabled.

### *How empowered are they?*

Rushing into negotiations without qualifying whether the other party is empowered to negotiate is a mistake many eager and ultimately frustrated account managers have made. The need to question, qualify and explore requires patience and an appreciation of the clarity this approach will provide. It is during this phase of initial discussions when the issue of empowerment should be qualified by simply asking, "are you in a position to sign off the agreement?" or "who else would you need to consult with as part of signing off this agreement?" or even "what limits are there which might prevent you from signing off the agreement?" All of these questions will help you to decide whether you are dealing with the right person or people.

### *Being disempowered*

Whether you open a bank account, take a driving test, buy a house, attend a court case or simply go to the gym, there are rules or laws stating what you can do, can't do and must do. If you break the rules or the law then you should expect the consequences and it is these parameters which we set that provide for civilized order. We are socially conditioned to conform and most of us lead our lives respecting the laws of where we live and others around us. Laws provide in some instances freedom of movement, for example effectively empowering us to travel and choose how and where we travel. Laws can also disempower us, in that we may not travel faster than a given speed or, when driving, having drunk alcohol and so on. When you enter an airport, check in your baggage, go through security and board the aeroplane, you are told what to do at every stage. If your bag is too heavy, you will have to pay more; going through passport control you need to have your bag scanned and remove your laptop, belt and so on; you may not move from your seat until the captain says that it's OK. In this environment, we are largely disempowered. The price of challenging these rules is to be evicted and potentially arrested.

The written word carries an assumed authority in that it has been published. It is designed to be legitimate. In a negotiation situation the other party might present you, say, with a price list. You may be tempted to accept this as it is, but it should be regarded as their opening position. Different situations require different considerations, yet many will wrongly assume that not only is the printed price fixed but the person issuing it is disempowered to negotiate.

The more empowered you are, the more scope you have with which to think and operate; the more scope to negotiate across broader agendas and the more opportunity to build valuable agreements. However, you will also become more exposed, carry more risk to your business and therefore be accountable for the total impact of your actions. Organizations have a tough challenge in providing a level of empowerment to their employees which helps the business conduct "good business" but not with such risks that the "good business" will eventually come at an unaffordable price.

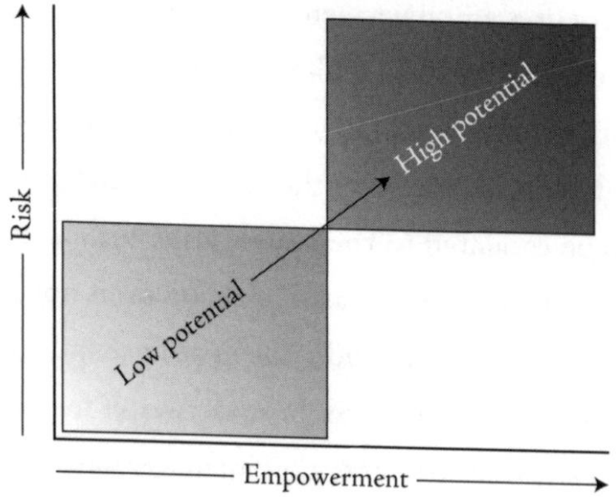


**Figure 7.1** Empowerment.

### *Fully empowered individuals can become very dangerous*

Rogue traders acting beyond their company's agreed levels of empowerment provide us with ample evidence of just how badly things can go wrong if scope, when provided, goes unchecked.

In 2007, Jerome Kerviel of Société Générale had taken up hedging positions that cost his business €4.9 billion in the biggest fraud in financial history. Other notable examples include Nick Leeson at Barings Bank, whose activities led to the bank, one of the oldest in the UK at the time, going out of business. Also there is Toshihide Iguchi at Japan's Daiwa Bank who cost his employers £1.1 billion, and John Rusnak at Allied Irish Bank who managed to lose his employers £335 million. These are just a few of the more well-publicized examples of what can happen when those who have been partially empowered operate outside the limits set, and without the necessary transparency and checks to protect everyone concerned.

### *Being partially empowered*

Every industry uses empowerment limits to protect their business. Call centres use this to make it almost impossible for customers to negotiate with their representatives who stick rigidly to their scripts. Any demand proposal made by the customer that sits outside the script has to be escalated to their supervisor – a classic avoidance strategy where the customer has to escalate or, if not, give up and concede. Other examples include: the insurance industry with the salesperson that can only refer to the underwriter for a decision, the shop assistant who has to refer to their manager when challenged by a customer and the hotel receptionist who has to check with their manager before agreeing to that special rate. Even the empowered negotiator may sometimes use the tactic of suggesting that their boss would not agree and therefore they cannot agree to the offer on the table.

In life we are surrounded by limits and rules, for the most part set in place to protect us from ourselves. For instance, a police officer can stop you, arrest you or take you into custody, but is not empowered to sentence you. That is the role of a judge who in turn is governed by the rule of law, the jury and the evidence. This process serves to prevent corruption and protects the system, whichever side of it you may be on. Within the context of a job, in the case of the police, they have the authority, responsibility and ultimately have been empowered to go so far in the apprehension process. What they can do and can't do as part of apprehending a suspect has been clearly defined in their training. It provides them with the confidence to escalate issues which are outside of their remit in the same way that you should operate with pre-agreed parameters within which you have been authorized.

## YOUR BOSS AS YOUR WORST ENEMY

The most dangerous person to take on the role of negotiator in any organization is the person with the most authority – usually the boss. The person who can say "yes" and knows that they are able to do so is more likely to do so and under pressure they often do. If you have ever attended a meeting alongside your boss you may well have experienced the following typical and yet frustrating scenario.

It is *your* client relationship but your boss wants to sit in for whatever reason. The meeting starts and you set out to discuss some of the challenging issues with your client, and then your boss starts to take over the conversation. In no time at all, your client and your boss are fully engaged in the discussion, they start exploring solutions and ultimately concessions are traded that you would not have been empowered to offer yourself. Your boss still thinks that they are doing the right thing and a great job at that. What has happened though is that your boss is as keen as you are to resolve the issue. They are however more empowered (which as we know, makes them more dangerous). Before long, your boss has concluded the meeting having built an agreement. Your boss has probably involved you along the way, yet may still have undermined your relationship and credibility with your client. Guess who the client asks to see at the next meeting?

Your boss may be highly skilled, have tremendous nerve and be very capable of managing relationships. However, they have a greater responsibility and accountability than you and therefore will be more exposed and will have more to lose if the deal deadlocks.

As they are most empowered, the boss is in the weakest negotiating position of anyone in your organization. Imagine your king in a game of chess. The king is not as mobile as the other pieces. If your king is "in check," you will always be vulnerable no matter how many pieces you have on the board. Therefore, your job is to protect your "king", to ensure that the other party do not gain access to them. In negotiation, your king is your boss and it is not in your interest to expose your boss directly to the other party, otherwise your team could find themselves in a compromised position. There is a famous mantra preached by buyers: "another level, another percent." The buyer will negotiate hard with their counterpart and then try to escalate to the next level to get that extra percent concession, and then escalate again for another percent and so on.

### *Who is in the background?*

If you are the boss it is in your interests to disempower yourself as this will protect you. Better to manage in the background and let the discussions unfold, than to be the focus of attention. Make it known that others will be taking the decisions and that you will back whatever decisions are taken.

In any negotiation, never assume that you are dealing with the ultimate decision maker. You may find yourself being enlightened at the end of your discussions, i.e. they have to refer the final decision to somebody else. The person you thought you were negotiating with was in fact not empowered to make the final decision. They may have also made offers that their business will not carry out. You may have even offered concessions in return for discount levels which the other person is ultimately not authorized to agree. Therefore it's imperative always to qualify the degree to which the other person is empowered.

- Establish who the decision maker is
- Establish who else will need to agree.

Do this before the negotiation begins. If not, you will leave yourself wide open to tactics, stalling, escalation or, worse still, agree to a contract which will not be delivered on, because the terms agreed were not viable.

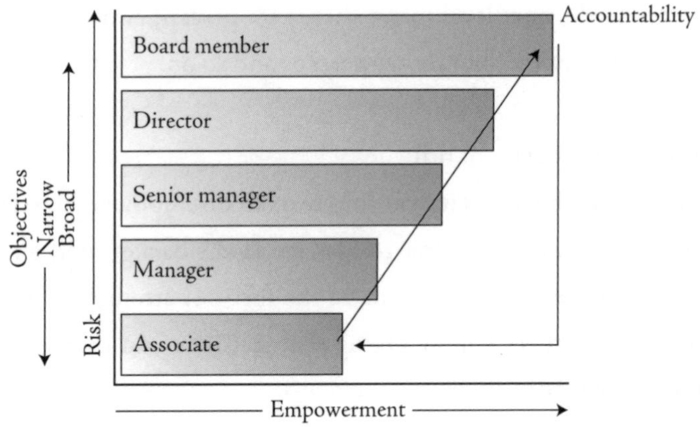


**Figure 7.2** Escalation.

### *Gaining "in principle" agreements*

Another way of using the boss to help negotiations flow where there is likely to be a high level of resistance is in arranging top-to-top meetings between senior management. These meetings are used to outline ideas and for gaining "in-principle" agreements, allowing for negotiations on the detail to follow up. This is used in both political and business environments as a means of protecting the boss from specific exposure, whilst allowing for trust and an understanding to be built between the two parties at a senior level.

The idea is that they are able to set in place some principles that provide for the smoother running of meetings, and defer to the negotiation teams to iron out the detail in future meetings. This method was used very effectively in the Northern Ireland peace process, where the parties would meet in "off the record meetings" in a bar at a hotel with a secret side entrance. This enabled the parties to agree in principle what the future might look like and to find common areas of agreement and to build trust. In 2010 in the UK, negotiations between the Conservative and Liberal Democrat political parties led to the formation of the coalition government after the hung parliament of the 2010 election. Neither party leader, David Cameron or Nick Clegg, were directly involved in negotiations. Both appointed a team to operate on their behalf and then to report back.

#### *The need to escalate to the empowered*

You may also consider using escalation as part of your negotiation strategy. This happens in retail stores every week.

**CASE STUDY**

A woman is looking at a sofa priced at $840. A salesman approaches her and attempts to close the sale by saying: "we can have it with you by next Saturday if you sign up today." The woman replies: "At this price, I would need to consult with my husband as we agreed not to go above $800." The salesman is already empowered (authorized) to discount by up to 10% on this sofa, and the woman is not apparently empowered to go above $800. The salesman qualifies this with his customer: "so if I could get my boss to agree to a price of $800 would you take it today?" knowing that he already has the authority. The woman nods. He asks her to wait, saying that he needs to speak with his manager. Following a short wait, he returns with a smile saying that he has been able to convince his manager to do the deal at $800, and they do the deal. But was the salesman really using empowerment to his advantage? Or was he being used by his customer's apparent disempowerment? The fact is that the woman might have been able to spend $1000 yet used her husband to disempower herself.

### *Broadening the negotiation scope by disempowering those at the top*

Another way to empower the negotiation process is for the broad strategies to be defined first by senior management.

**CASE STUDY**

Celino, a sheet glass distribution company based in Poland, had decided to renegotiate a new set of terms with the 37 existing customers they had across Europe. The changes that required renegotiation included prices, volumes, discount structures, information sharing, payment terms and order lead times.

Ultimately, their customers would be paying more for their sheet glass, some of which were of a commodity nature and some of which were provided with unique properties, for example self-cleaning coatings over which they held exclusivity. They knew the negotiations were going to be tough. However, 80% of their business was with their five largest customers so the size and importance of these customers were the primary focus for the leaders of the business.

The strategy adopted by Celino involved top-to-top meetings to discuss new exclusive innovative coatings, reliability of delivery lead times and uniform transparent pricing across the market. These messages were sold without mention of specific details. During their meetings the directors would not be drawn on the specific changes to terms on the basis that they did not have the information down to product level. They insisted that both parties had teams who could work through "the detail." They focused on reliability and the benefits of how the new innovative products would help their customers' businesses grow, both of which their customers felt positive towards, be it at this early stage.

Essentially, they had paved the way for negotiations by disempowering themselves and by not becoming drawn on details. Had they not done so they would have compromised their strategy.

## NEGOTIATION USING EMPOWERMENT WITHIN TEAM ROLES

When negotiating in teams it is important to be organized in such a way that you perform well as a unit. Understanding who is empowered to do what and who will take the final decisions is also key to the workings of any team in pressured situations. Negotiating in teams can only be effective when everyone understands their role, that is if everyone is disciplined enough to keep to their role and is able to contribute towards the team's efforts. There are four distinct team roles which are typically adopted:

- the spokesperson
- the figures person
- the observer
- the leader.

Each is designed to help your team perform to the best of its varied abilities.

### The spokesperson

The spokesperson is empowered to conduct most of the dialogue, including tabling proposals within the parameters set out by their boss or in this case the leader in the negotiation team. That is not to say that others should not or cannot talk but they should do so through invitation from the spokesperson. Within their role, the spokesperson is empowered to trade on behalf of the team, yet will need to refer to their leader to get final agreement.

### The figures person

The figures person understands the implications of movement on each of the variables. They are in the team to advise on possibilities, calculate movements and proposals, and understand the total value of the agreement at any given point in time. They should be disempowered to make commitments or enter the dialogue in the meeting unless invited to do so.

### The observer

The observer is also disempowered. Their role is to:

- watch and monitor the other party;
- hear the things that others may be too preoccupied to hear;
- read the size, timing and nature of the moves which are taking place.

The purpose of the role is to help you to understand what is driving the other party. The observer is your informer in the room but is not empowered to negotiate.

#### The leader

The leader sets out the agenda and forms the climate for the meeting. They allow the spokesperson to manage the trading on behalf of the team. The leader or the boss is usually the person with the greatest level of authority. They are the person who speaks least, but speaks loudest. The leader will summarize from time to time where clarity is required and make the final decision. However, they are not the negotiator. This task is delegated to the spokesperson who is the voice piece of the team.

The team are there to support the spokesperson.

### *More than four*

Often the team is larger than four members. More frequently, you will have to play all four roles yourself, at the same time. This makes your task of negotiating more demanding because there are many things to think about, consider and respond to. This is one of the reasons why preparation is so important to negotiators. You should never think on your feet, never seek to rush the deal, and always understand the pace at which you can operate and manage your meetings accordingly.

For some, disempowerment feels like a straitjacket, for others, a suit of armor. It works both ways and is used by companies to expand or narrow the scope and risk. It is used as a tactic to protect or deflect conflict, as well as a negotiating lever.

Even a pilot landing their aircraft will take instructions from air traffic control regarding flight path, timings and other relevant instructions during descent. They are part of a team and different members of the team will carry different forms of responsibility and will be empowered to make certain decisions. Fortunately, everything the pilot does can be seen by everyone who has an interest in their activity.

## GETTING EMPOWERED BEFORE YOU START

You probably already work within agreed parameters when negotiating. Without those parameters, you could in theory become dangerous because you could agree to anything. So, degrees of empowerment are usually put in place to protect you (providing you with a basis for trading), and to protect your businesses. Often before negotiations start, you may find yourself involved in internal negotiations to discuss your parameters by agreeing what your break point is, or whether you will entertain discussions on particular variables as part of concluding the deal. This is an important part of the planning process. Equally, the other party will have parameters within which they can operate. It is quite common for some people to open a negotiation discussion outlining the areas that are non-negotiable "deal breakers" and the areas which are available for discussion. The likelihood is that they are either not empowered to negotiate over certain areas because of the parameters which have been set, or they have decided for now to introduce such parameters, allowing them to broaden the agenda during later discussions.

## EMPOWERMENT WHICH PROTECTS YOU

Many organizations actively promote such business values as creativity, entrepreneurship and even empowerment. This serves to encourage open thinking and promote an unconstrained culture. Yet when negotiating with suppliers and customers they recognize that there have to be limits within which individuals are empowered to operate, otherwise the business will lose total control of its operation. The same businesses that promote these values also operate a disempowered structure to protect their own business operation. They use a price list which serves to disempower the salesperson, as does the accompanying printed discount structure. It is defended on the basis of providing transparent pricing for all and that volumes can be accommodated in the accompanying discount structure but no more. The salesperson under these circumstances is disempowered to the point where they are little more than an order taker. If the customer demands better terms they have to speak to the boss. The boss, a supervisor, is also disempowered. They have a boss and if you can get to them, because they are usually "out of town," you may just be able to negotiate a better deal.

Tactically, empowerment allows you to use a third party, citing your lack of authority to move further, which serves to take the pressure away from you. If not used carefully though, it can backfire. Many companies employ an escalation process involving many layers of empowerment, ensuring those they negotiate with never really get to the ultimate decision maker.

**CASE STUDY**

The seller says: "If you can agree to a price of $19 a unit on 30 days delivery, we will agree to payment terms of 30 days." The buyer says "I am able to agree to that, but I just need to run that past my boss as it is above my authorization level, I'll call you this afternoon." That afternoon, the buyer calls the salesman: "Good news, my boss says that if you can agree to $18 a unit he will sign it off." The salesman sees this as a tactic they have come across before, called "Defence in Depth." However, he needs the deal, so yields to the offer: "OK, but I need a confirmation in writing back by the morning." "That's great," says the buyer, "We can now put the agreement before the head of buying for the final sign-off and I'll have it back to you by the morning." The following morning arrives and the buyer calls the seller. "The head of buying says that if the deal meets our standard payment terms of 45 days, he will sign the agreement. Of course I would have signed it off, but it's out of my hands now." The seller is so close and because he is empowered to authorize the 45 days, he agrees, "Just sign it and get it back to me."

The pressure the salesman is under to get the agreement signed, and the fact that he works for an "empowering" sales organization, has resulted in the salesman's position being compromised. Had he been disempowered to move beyond certain predefined limits, the buyer may well have had to review his approach or renegotiated on other variables. This higher authority tactic is used frequently where one party does not qualify the decision-making process beyond the person they are dealing with, leaving themselves exposed to further negotiations.

## EMPOWERED TO DO THE WRONG THINGS?

Some retailers who have set objectives for their product buyers based on gross margin growth carry this same risk. Gross margin is calculated before many of the costs associated with receiving the product have been taken into account.

Imagine you are a retail buyer. Your objective across the category of products you are responsible for is to increase your average gross margin from 37% to 38.5% this year. Now imagine the temptation to offer those things to your suppliers which do not reflect on your gross margin, including logistics arrangements, forward orders, and even special promotions in your quest to improve your gross margin. You may actually sell less product, taking less money and making less profit, but as long as your gross margin goes up you will have achieved your objective. Narrow individual objectives drive behavior and if you are empowered to operate across all of the necessary terms and yet are not measured on the total performance, the decisions you take will reflect those things you are measured on rather than results that can be detrimental to your employer.

Many buyers of products from around the world will use agents to source goods or materials. The agents will identify suppliers and negotiate with them on your behalf. But how do you know they are getting the best deal on your behalf, or that you are even getting the best deal from them? Empowering agents on your behalf requires careful management as they will also be looking for ways to make a living.

## DECISION-MAKING AUTHORITY

### *Being empowered by your customer*

Gaining access to talk, to sell and negotiate across larger organizations can be a challenge. Many of us have to negotiate for the privilege of preferred status with customers who are effectively saying if you agree to our terms, we will authorize or empower you to discuss terms in an exclusive manner across the rest of our business. Until then the people you need to talk to are disempowered even to talk to you. The local regional or country operators will have effectively been told not to entertain discussions (they are disempowered) until a preferred supplier agreement is in place.

Empowerment essentially means the authority to negotiate. This ranges from the shop assistant who has no scope to negotiate over the price displayed and will simply escalate any discussions on the subject to their manager, to the other extreme, where the business owner who is selling their business can agree to any terms which they feel inclined to. Although having worked hard to create their business, they may still need to explain their decisions to their spouse or family. And then there are the varying degrees to the amount to which one can be empowered.

#### CASE STUDY

Imagine your boss empowers you to complete a deal selling water dispensers, but that you are not to go below $300 a unit, unless you speak to them first. In this instance, they would then know that unless they hear from you, the deal will be done for no less than $300 a unit, all other things remaining equal. $300 becomes your break point (the point beyond which you are not authorized to agree). Empowerment can work both for you and against you by being too narrow. In this example it may work against you if, for instance, you return with a deal for $320 a unit. However, in order to secure $320 a unit, you have agreed to deliver within 3 days (usually 2 weeks), to payment terms of 60 days (usually 7 days) and to a minimum order of 10 units (usually 30).

By capping or limiting one variable (price to no less than $300), the other variables have been manipulated, resulting in a deal that is actually worth less than the $300 a unit agreed. On the other hand, imagine you are offered a deal by a large company for 500 units, but they insist that you offer a price of $290. Rather than refer, you deadlock and lose what would have been a highly profitable deal. So, absolute instructions regarding authority on any one issue should be explained, along with conditions outlining when referral or escalation should take place.

***Linking empowerment to accountability and risk assessment***

The year 2006 witnessed the accelerated use of "e-auctions" supported by an industry which provided the "e-auction" support services, meaning that just about anything could be sourced using this online approach. This involved inviting suppliers to bid in a competitive environment for orders. They would be in competition with each other in a bidding war aimed at attracting reduced pricing, mainly on commodity-based items. During 2006 "e-auctions" were delivering retailers average savings in excess of 20%. Decisions were quickly taken to roll the "e-auction" model out across a wider range of product categories.

### CASE STUDY

One such product was a large grocer buying shopping trolleys – 250,000 of them, in fact – via an e-auction. A supplier from Taiwan put forward their latest trolley which met the specification outlined by the grocer. Another supplier in Italy put forward their trolley which also met the specification.

Unknown at this stage however was that the trolley made in Taiwan was built to last for three years whereas the Italian model was designed for a life of six years. Life expectancy was not stipulated in the original specification ahead of bidding.

The supplier from Taiwan was awarded the contract and of course generated the 20% saving for the grocer. However, after three years, the wheels needed replacing and brake mechanisms started to fail and they needed to be replaced, incurring huge additional costs to replace all 250,000 trolleys – a false economy, especially as the cost of the trolleys was to be written off over five years.

Had the negotiators carried long-term accountability as a variable, the specification may have been more detailed. They had delegated the role of the bidding process to an outside agency, empowering them to get the best price, which they did. The specification had not been thought through, the agency acted as directed which resulted in a total value deal which simply lacked long-term value for the purchaser. Within three years, the buyer responsible had already moved into a more senior position, partly on the basis of some of the strong cost savings they had delivered – including the trolley auction.

## CASE STUDY

In another case a manufacturer was involved in a negotiation to supply safety helmets for a new construction site. Their contact was a procurement manager who needed to place an order for two sizes of helmet that had to be made to meet specific health and safety standards.

- The safety helmets were being purchased to be worn on a new construction site due to accommodate over 700 contractors.
- The helmets needed to be delivered on site within four weeks when the contractors were due to arrive and the next health and safety inspection was due.
- The owners of the site managed a number of other sites, some of which were due to be started in the next few months.

The procurement manager had narrowed down the potential suppliers to two known manufacturers and then commenced his negotiations. The first supplier offered a very keen price, subject to preferred supplier status and a guaranteed order to supply the remaining four other sites to be launched, at the same price per unit. The second supplier did not ask for the longer-term order, were 5% more expensive and could not deliver for five weeks.

The procurement manager's instincts were to go with the first offer. However, he then considered what risks might this entail? The first supplier was cheaper but what were the implications if they were to deliver late? The costs could be hundreds of times the price of the order. He double-checked the specification, trying to work out why they were so cheap. What would the implications be of the hats not meeting specification when they arrive? The sample helmets seemed OK. However, the risks to the site not being operational because of failure to meet the health and safety requirements meant this deal was not just about the hats. It was about the total site being ready to operate, and that meant the hats being ready and available to wear. The procurement manager referred to his boss to discuss the merits of the options. Ultimately they requested written guarantees from both suppliers and recognition of the consequences of late delivery. Not surprisingly, only the second supplier responded and so secured the order.

The difference between these two case studies – the attitudes of the key negotiators to risk and therefore total value – is accountability. Any individual who is empowered to negotiate the best deal must also be made accountable for the broader implications of their agreements; otherwise what appears like a great deal could turn out to be a disaster for the organization. The challenge for the empowered negotiator is therefore to understand and negotiate/mitigate for the risks and, when in doubt, escalate.

## EMPOWERMENT AND SCOPE TO CREATE VALUE

So, responsibility and accountability go hand in hand. Some businesses want their managers to be entrepreneurial. They want to empower them to take decisions, to be creative, to build agreements and to maximize value within the agreements they are involved in.

In fact, high potential deals come from creative thinking (trait 9, Chapter 4, page 118). Creative thinking comes from those who are empowered and therefore encouraged to think more broadly. If you disempower someone by providing them with limited scope to operate, it will limit their thinking and attract responses such as: "I didn't even consider the prospect of a joint venture; it's not part of my remit."

If you want to negotiate incremental value in your agreements you need to be empowered with as much scope as possible.

#### *The importance of defining value*

Having greater scope with moderate forms of empowerment is a healthy way of balancing behavior within the organization. However, scope and creativity must also be linked to accountability. You might ask someone to build creative deals that maximize value. However, unless you define *how* value will be measured they may overlook the risks they have accepted in their quest to extract value. If the personal benefits associated with highly profitable agreements are very high, limits of authority may be worth building into the negotiator's brief. As we have witnessed in the global banking industry in the lead up to the credit crunch during 2008/9, individuals will entertain risk in the quest for personal gain, especially when they are authorized to do so.

# CHAPTER 8

# Tactics and Values

## THE IMPORTANCE OF BEING DISPASSIONATE

The decisions you take and the way you behave during your negotiations will be influenced by how much power you think you have and by the way your own values or ethics shape your judgement.

It is also true that the tactics you choose to use in your negotiations will firstly be limited by how much power you have and whether you have a short- or long-term relationship to consider. This in turn may influence how ethical you choose to be during your negotiations.

You may regard trust, respect, integrity, honesty, openness, consideration, compassion and empathy as important social values, but at the point where you convert these into a desire to be fair in negotiation your judgement and your deals can become compromised (see page 179, Chapter 6).

The dilemma of where the value of fairness fits into negotiation has challenged many. For instance, some organizations who hold strong views on being fair and reasonable, when faced with a trading partner who behaves in a manipulative or irrational manner, take exception to the conduct. They will on principle not tolerate the behavior and will exit the relationship. But how much of this is business principle and how much is an emotional reaction? Have you ever become irritated or even antagonized to the point where you decide to walk away from discussions when the other party is being "unfair", even though there was a deal to be done?

Ultimately, you cannot afford to allow your emotions to influence your judgement in negotiation. Try to be dispassionate and to recognize the tactics in play used by others. You need to detach what, or even *who*, you are (partly formed by your values) from *what* you do. This does not mean abandoning your values but simply recognizing how your values can make you become principled, which can become the undoing of your ability to perform.

### *Recognizing the process and the gamesmanship in play*

As a Complete Skilled Negotiator you need to accept that the other party's behavior has to be kept in check; otherwise your ability to think clearly will be clouded and your decision-making ability affected.

Importantly, you need to recognize that the other party may not share your values or views on how to conduct business and may have come to the negotiation table with a completely different game plan in mind.

Negotiating is not about fairness, but it is about working towards an agreement which both parties are prepared to commit to and remain motivated enough to fulfil.

Because of the way the balance of power is split, and how it can change with time and circumstance, means you cannot expect agreements always to be, or appear to be, balanced and fair, or even consistent. You can, however, work towards getting the best possible deal given the circumstances you face. Some, faced with such situations, turn to tactics to help them; some become victims of the tactics in play. The Complete Skilled Negotiator sees them for what they are and where necessary uses counter tactics to neutralize their effects.

I am not implying here what is right or wrong. You will have values that are probably different from those of others'. This does not make yours right or wrong; it does not make the other party's values right or wrong. It will simply mean that our interpretation, understanding and use of tactics will differ as the implications of making use of them will differ based on our circumstances and our view of what acceptable behavior is made up of.

As a general rule, negotiations which focus on short-term agreements with parties with whom we have no ongoing relationship, or prospect of one in the future, are more inclined to gravitate towards value distribution (1–6 o'clock) negotiations. Tactics tend to be more readily used in these styles of negotiations as the relationships involved tend not to be long term.

## A QUESTION OF CHOICES AND PERSONAL STYLE

Our social values are influenced by history, politics, religion, family and social groups. They provide a basis for civilization. The value of fairness provides us with a consistent basis to judge, debate and agree decisions and a framework for people with different views to manage their lives. Political parties have even been known to campaign for a "fairer society," as if to suggest that this will make for a better society. This "fairness" will, however, be relative to the interests and the power already held by those involved.

The concept of "fairness" is exploited by some negotiators through the use of tactics. Western democratic societies are designed to offer freedom and choice. This serves to remove the notion of being controlled, and, as long as we have choices, many perceive this as freedom and fairness. So choices are designed to signal fairness. However, if like governments, you are *controlling* the options or choices, then you have the power to influence the outcome.

When we are given a menu in a restaurant we feel that we are being given a choice and have control over the meal that we will eat. We would not have entered the restaurant had we not liked the choice on the menu. However, the choice is still ultimately limited to the selection that the chef has put before us. It is our choice to engage. In negotiation it is the agenda which is developed, providing the choice of altering the terms associated with the featured variables; the offer to move payment terms (but only if you accept the price increase and agree today) is a choice.

However, if you are overtly unfair in the choices you provide, others, trust will be difficult to build and, with no trust, it is difficult to sustain strategic partners, or to negotiate collaboratively (7–12 o'clock on the clock face).

Social laws or the unwritten laws of society help us to determine what is fair and reasonable under whatever circumstances. Business partnerships, where there is a need to maintain productive relationships and the need to jointly problem-solve or develop incremental value by working together, requires at least some level of trust.

To be perceived to be fair in business, one needs to offer choices: choices which are not so extreme that they quickly become regarded as unfair.

### *Personal attributes*

Your personal values and how they influence your behavior will have a powerful bearing on where you and the other party gravitates to on the clock face. They can, if not managed, directly influence whether you build relationships or whether you enter into combat each time you seek to agree terms. Below are some of the personal attributes to consider and the influence they will exert during your negotiations.

**Trust** in business has to be earned and is easily broken. It implies that you are good for your word. If you say something will happen, it happens, consistently. You approach the conversation from their perspective, sharing their concerns and working on the problems that you both identify, together. It does not mean that you have to pay by conceding on terms, offering personal favors or by being more transparent with your interests.

**Respect** comes from being firm. If you are too flexible or concede too easily, the other party will regard you as being weak and are less likely to want to do business with you. In negotiation, everything is possible, but difficult. The fact that it is difficult ensures that the work you put into the deal, engineering the terms, and moving reluctantly, attracts respect for you, the other party and the deal you finish with.

**Integrity** comes from consistency. This can present issues for negotiators who are too focused on not being unpredictable. Maintaining confidentiality with information and being reliable, in that you follow through with your commitments, will also help promote integrity, which in some relationships or even industries is critical if business is to take place at all. Some companies prize themselves highly on their integrity in how they work and operate; they invest in offices, building marble hallways and strong architecture to enhance the impression of the longevity that they have, both in business and by association in their relationships with clients.

**Honesty**. You never need lie in negotiation. You don't even have to tell them what you won't do. Focus on what you will do. Think "how" or "on what basis could we, or could they?" To remain consistent, you need to maintain honesty. By telling them you are prepared to pay $100 when you know that you could pay $150 is not lying. You are simply telling them what you are prepared to pay. Don't confuse the process of negotiation with lying and telling the truth. If you lie in negotiation, you could be taking unnecessary risks and in some cases completely compromising relationships and the basis upon which your business conducts itself, but don't expect everyone to adhere to this discipline.

**Consideration** of the needs of the other party. If you don't understand these you are not ready to negotiate. Your planning, preparation, research, exploration meetings are all there to help you to establish their position, motives, priorities and interests. To place a value on these you have to understand the deal the way they do from inside their head. Considering the facts will allow you to remain sensitive to the issues and respectful where necessary.

**Empathy** with the other party's position can help you to work out other ways of packaging the deal. The more you understand about their position, priorities and needs, the better positioned you are to negotiate with them. Never feel sorry for them or obligated to help them. Empathy is about understanding and appreciating the challenges from their perspective, but never compromising because of such understandings.

**Responsibility.** It is you who will conduct your negotiations and you who will make the decisions with the authority limits you have been given. The more trust that genuinely exists within your relationships, the more scope you have to open up the agenda and work together creatively. This will only come about if you cultivate the necessary climate and discussions. Often, the only issue between companies conducting business more profitably is the personalities in play. You have to take responsibility for the relationship and the chemistry between those involved if the negotiation is going to deliver incremental value.

### *Risky attributes*

**Openness.** This can be dangerous in negotiation. Information is power and the more you share with the other party, the more you will expose yourself. However, there will always be information that you can or would want to share, if only for the purpose of positioning or anchoring the other party. Be open but stay within the parameters that you set yourself. If you don't understand this from the outset you will place yourself in a very vulnerable position.

**Generosity** engenders greed in negotiation. Everything should be traded and conditional if it is to be respected and valued. Generosity simply does not have a place in the negotiation process. The more you give, the more they will want. For this reason alone, every trade must be conditional or at the very least a considered, conscious, commercial decision. It could be called an "investment." You may also lose the respect of the other party for giving away unconditional concessions and, most certainly in the short term, will suboptimize your opportunity.

**Compassion.** In the tough world of business your job is to maximize opportunity. You will do this with those you can work with, rely on and who remain highly competitive. This is a capitalist market we operate in. Compassion, like generosity, has to take a back seat once a negotiation commences unless of course you have a longer-term plan in mind.

## WHAT ARE TACTICS?

### *When do tactics usually come into play?*

Tactics, although not exclusively, tend to be used more when one party has more power than the other and tries to take advantage of it. Tactics are also more frequently used where the nature of the negotiation is based on value distribution and the focus is on taking as much value off the table as possible.

### *Dealing with tactics and when to use them*

There are dozens of books written on negotiation which present tactics as the basis of negotiation. They are given names which serve to explain the approach: "The Russian Front," "The Trojan Horse," and so on. The most important thing about tactics is to recognize them for what they are.

- They are neither clever nor sophisticated.
- They are designed to apply pressure and usually by those who can because they have enough power to do so, or those who think they are clever enough to do so without any consequences.

However, they are used with such regularity that one has to recognize and understand them, adapt to them and, where necessary, even use them, where appropriate. To help with this I have categorized a range of tactics using a simple scale of 1–10 (1 is low and 10 is high) against two factors:

- **Power required:** the amount of power you will need to have or be perceived to have relative to the other party for this tactic to work.
- **Relationship erosion:** the degree to which your relationship or any trust that may exist within it will be eroded, if the tactic once used becomes obvious or transparent to the other party.

For the purpose of outlining some of the more widely used tactics, I have placed them into one of seven categories. These are:

1. Information
2. Time and momentum
3. Fear or guilt
4. Anchoring
5. Empowerment
6. Moving the costs around
7. Deceit.

### 1. Information

Information is power. The more information you have about the options, circumstances and priorities of the other party, the more powerful you become.

***"The hypothetical question"*** *(Power required 1, Relationship erosion 1)*

"What if" and "Suppose that" questions used during the exploratory and closing stages can help to work out the degree of flexibility the other party is prepared to offer, or the relative value of the issues being discussed.

For example "What if we were to 'hypothetically' increase the order after three months, how might that change the fee structure?" There may be no intention of doing so, but the idea is to understand the scope for fee reduction or other changes for reference later during the negotiation. "What if we were unable to meet your payment schedule?" Again, the idea is to test flexibility and to establish how important this variable is. It allows you to test assumptions and trade more effectively later on during discussions. The hypothetical question technique can be used to explore possibilities, especially where deadlock is looming. However, be careful that this does not backfire. Asking such questions can gain you some insights but their value may be cancelled out if the question is turned back on you.

***"Off the record"*** *(Power required 1, Relationship erosion 2)*

This is the next information-based tactic where one party asks the other for a view, a comment, or to simply share an insight, in the name of helping both parties make progress. Their intentions may be genuine, but the information sought is sought for one reason only: to get inside your head. You may choose to use it yourself for the same reason. However, when asked for an off the record meeting, always remember the real risks you carry. Any indications, signal, comments or even attitudes you imply towards their comments will be read into. As far as you are concerned, in the true sense of the term, there is no such thing as an "off the record" meeting. Anything you tell them or their business will quickly make its way to the decision maker and is likely to influence the decision making of the other party. By all means make use of "off the record," but do not get used by it.

***Full disclosure and openness*** *(Power required 3, Relationship erosion 3)*
When a request for full disclosure is made before or during a meeting, there needs to be a reasonable degree of trust or mutual dependency before parties tend to agree. Even then it tends to come with conditions or limits: "We will share our data with you on the current site, but feel that extending this to our overall operation to be unnecessary," is the type of response you will get. Some will say: "I'm going to be really open with you," which usually means they are not. This is also the case when people use such words as "really," "actually," "genuinely," "seriously," "sincerely" and, most common of all, "honestly." Whenever I have heard these words in negotiation where people are under pressure, I have concluded that the truth has not been in play.

We are conditioned from a very early age in life to believe that lying is wrong so, subconsciously, such words are used to sell the very proposals that others are unconvinced by.

In doing so, this highlights the lack of soundness or truth in that which is being stated. Listen out for them and remain mindful of the longer-term implications of full disclosure.

Even when two parties are working very closely together, for example on a joint venture, it is still possible that full disclosure may have a different meaning to one party than to the other.

When one party offers to provide open-book costings, understand what is not being provided as well as what is. In reality, you can assume that something will usually be held back. The process of due diligence is used for very good reasons: to ensure the integrity of information provided is true and complete.

**Why?** *(Power required 1, Relationship erosion 1)*

This simple question can be used to challenge everything from agenda items to new proposals. It has been proved as an effective way of establishing the thinking and importance of any issue or statement. Anyone can ask "why?", which is why curious children ask it time after time in their quest for knowledge. The information you receive will always provide an insight, even if it's something like: "We are not prepared to go into detail on that issue." During exploration discussions, it's worth asking why the other party is asking the very question that they are; and what insight does this give me into their thinking?

### 2. Time and momentum

Time is the most powerful lever available to any negotiator. Time and circumstances affect the value of just about every product or service bought and sold around the world. The value, from the perspective of both parties, changes sometimes dramatically with time. If the product does not arrive on time, it loses its value; if the service cannot be provided when it is needed, it loses its value. If I were going to provide you with a full advertising plan to support your election campaign and the election was due to be held in June, but I could not start until June, my services would be deemed useless and without value. However, if the service could kick in during March, and run for three months peaking with tailored activity throughout June, the service may attract a premium. It's the same service with a different time slot, which makes all the difference. So, understanding the time pressures of the other party is vital to you being able to optimize the leverage during your negotiations. How you communicate your own time pressures or use the other party's time pressures to gain movement or agreement can be directly influenced by the tactics you use.

***Deadlines*** *(Power required 5, Relationship erosion 3)*

"If you do not agree by Friday we will not be able to start the project in the timescales you have stipulated."

"We are closing the book on this one so we will need to know by this afternoon if you want to take part."

"If we can agree in principle today, I will ensure you get the business, subject to us 'ironing out' the terms."

The pressure that deadlines can exert means that negotiators not only use the tactic as a closing device, but also to provide you with the feeling of having "won." Deadlines are used in many other ways, for example: "Because of changes in our business, after today's deadline, any agreement will have to be signed off by my boss." On some occasions, once the other party has established your deadlines (stipulating an agreement required this month for example), they will employ this need as a trading variable. They will imply that the timing issue is not so critical to them. Be careful when providing total transparency relating to the implications of deadlines; it can be a highly effective and manipulative tool.

***"And just one more thing"*** *(Power required 4, Relationship erosion 6)*

This is often used at the end of the negotiation when the deal is regarded as all but done. One party turns to the other just as you are about to shake hands and says: "Just one more thing, you will of course be including the flexible payment scheduling we discussed earlier?" They pause and wait with their hand held out. You think, I'm there, deal done, finished, closed. Do I now open up the discussion again, or worse still, compromise the agreement by saying "no, but I didn't think that flexible payment scheduling was ever part of the terms I thought we had agreed?"

Many less experienced negotiators at this stage yield and concede, using whatever justification they choose for doing so. "I wasn't going to jeopardize a million euro agreement for a five hundred euro concession at the end." The party using the "And just one more thing" are implying a misunderstanding through the attitude of "we thought that was included." As you can see, this tactic has a higher relationship erosion factor. If the other party has either power or enough nerve, they will and should challenge the assumption by attaching a condition to the flexible payment scheduling in the same way they would have, as if it had been used earlier during the formal discussions. If the other party has genuinely overlooked an issue, even following the summarizing of positions, they will generally accept that a further trade-off may be necessary. If not, it is a tactical ploy.

***Denied access*** *(Power required 7, Relationship erosion 9)*

When you need to move discussions on, perhaps under some time pressure, or there may be obvious implications to you if certain deadlines pass and the other party knows that the longer the discussions go on, the weaker your position will become, some will use denied access as a tactic. They simply ensure they are not available. They tell their colleagues and assistants to pass on the message they are in back-to-back meetings, out of town, away, or anything which ensures that you, the other party, cannot make progress until they are ready.

This is often used in conjunction with a time deadline. You are waiting to get sign-off on your promotion from your buyer. They know you need their company to participate for the national promotion to be viable. They know you have a cut-off date of Monday so they employ denied access until Monday, with the assumption that you will be more accommodating of their demands than you would have been on the previous Wednesday. Or perhaps it's your month end and an important order will make the difference between you making your target and missing it. The other party is aware that it's your month end so stall, making themselves unavailable until the last minute and then return to you with last-minute demands. One way of dealing with this situation when you are confident that denied access is in play is to leave a message for the other party, bringing your deadline artificially forward, adding that if the deadline passes without agreement, the deal is off or the terms on offer are diminished. This, although risky, buys you a window of opportunity between the deadline they think you are working to and the one actually in play. Another is to introduce a credible option, perhaps another party or option that you plan to take up and you need to let them know within certain timescales. If you don't hear back you will place the order, reluctantly, elsewhere. Of course these options carry risks but often work as a way of unlocking the denied access tactic.

***Time constraint*** *(Power required 6, Relationship erosion 6)*
This is used where the other party introduces artificial time lines or deadlines, stating that their offer expires on a certain date. Further demands are then introduced as a consequence of the deadline not being met as "compensation" against the implications.

Time constraints are also used where one party is near agreement on most of the terms, but the other decides to hold out for a better fee rate. They say: "We will give you one last chance to increase your offer. Please advise us by 5.30 pm on Friday of what this is, and we will let you know if we are prepared to progress." During the time that passes, which is aimed at fuelling uncertainty and doubt, the other party is often pressured into improving their final offer.

***The Auction*** *(Power required 5, Relationship erosion 3)*

The bidding process is designed to create competition. The process is engineered and controlled by the organizers. As the bids increase, rational judgement is in danger of being put to one side as, for those with high egos, winning can take over as the predominant driver of behavior. Time and momentum work against those willing to continue bidding, so a clear and absolute break point must feature as part of your planning if you are to enter such a process.

***Time out*** *(Power required 1, Relationship erosion 1)*

When in doubt, for whatever reason, adjourn the meeting and take a time out to regroup. You need to understand the implications, risks or finances if you are to maintain clarity and be able to work out how you are going to move forward. It is often used when new information comes to the fore or if deadlock is looming and a need for a "fresh look" at the deal is needed. It's also used when time is running out and one party chooses to put the other under pressure by removing themselves from the room until time pressures become critical.

### 3. Fear or guilt

This next category raises the stakes in the relationship and heightens the risk. With high levels of power, threats are used in subtle ways to create movement. It is the fear of these threats or the fear of losing the deal which is played upon by those seeking to manipulate the power they have.

***Physically disturbing them*** *(Power required 10, Relationship erosion 10)*
This is made up of a variety of non-violent but yet physical gestures which are introduced to unsettle and distract you. This can include leaning across the table to invade your personal space, sitting very close to you, or changing the seating pattern, so they are sat next to you. Seating positioned to face the sunlight, or groups crammed into very small rooms are all part of the environment used to intimidate. Remember, you are in charge and that includes your environment, so if it does not feel right, challenge it, question it and change it. You'll attract respect for doing so and set the scene for equal respect in the meeting.

***Good guy, bad guy*** *(Power required 7, Relationship erosion 9)*
Typically used in team negotiations where one member of the team makes very high or irrational demands, and the other offers a more reasonable approach, or one is challenging and dismissive whilst their colleague presents themselves as far more understanding. The approach is designed to make the "good guys" appear reasonable, rational and understanding, and therefore all the more agreeable. Essentially it's using the law of relativity to attract cooperation. It's transparent enough and certainly erodes any potential for trust, so ensure next time you are exposed to it that you see it for what it is.

***The Russian Front*** *(Power required 8, Relationship erosion 6)*
The other party presents you with two options. The first is initially unacceptable; the second is so bad that under no circumstances would you consider it. It represents just about the worst thing that could happen. As described by Gavin Kennedy in his book *Everything is Negotiable*, this tactic is taken from the Second World War where a Russian lieutenant was told by his colonel that he would be sent to the Russian Front unless he did as asked. The colonel had the power, the lieutenant believed it was for real and the result was predictable. He would do whatever was asked willingly, rather than being sent to the Russian Front. In negotiation, it is used when providing two options. One you know will prove unprofitable, and the other would be an outright disaster. If the whole concept is not rejected, the chances are you will be seduced into agreeing to the "bad one."

***Personal favor*** *(Power required 4, Relationship erosion 4)*
This tactic attempts to make the position or request "personal" and works most effectively in familiar relationships: "You can do this for old times' sake," or "If you do this for me I will ensure your proposal is accepted," or "You scratch my back and I'll scratch yours." It leans on a sense of obligation to the point where it's aimed at leaving you feeling embarrassed if you do not yield. You must remain firm, point out the compromising position this would leave you in and explain that it's not personal, just business.

***Guilty party*** *(Power required 4, Relationship erosion 6)*
This involves suggesting that the other party is breaking some code or agreement, or that they are going against the industry norm, or that a commitment has not been met or a performance not as

it should be. This tactic is used to full effect where one party is negotiating compensation to include inconvenience, loss of face, indirect loss of earnings, even future risk; this results in a demand way beyond the normal financial obligations.

***The social smell*** *(Power required 3, Relationship erosion 3)*
The social smell is used to imply that you are the odd one out. It's designed to make you question your own judgement: "if everyone else is behaving in a certain way (agreeing) why am I not?" It comes in the form of a statement about what "others are doing" and importantly what you are not. It implies that you are out of sync, the odd one out and that you are missing out or even being irrational. "Everyone else has committed … you'll be the only one not included so you are likely to miss out whilst your competitors have all agreed." The idea is that it helps apply pressure to conform, highlights isolation and promotes self-doubt.

***Silence*** *(Power required 1, Relationship erosion 3)*
As a powerful tactic, silence is used to unnerve the other party. It can result in a waiting game because the first to talk is likely to be the first to concede. For many, the discomfort alone of continued silence can result in a concession. Silence is uncomfortable; so much so that many are tempted to fill the void by talking and, in doing so, they offer further flexibility or end up offering concessions. Anything to make the dreaded silence go away. And yet for the experienced negotiator it may be that they simply need time to think through their next move. Silence is best used directly after you have stated your proposal or after they have stated theirs. Just wait. Even if they respond, wait further. The pressure builds and often leads to more concessions.

4. Anchoring

The fourth category of tactics is where one party sets out to form an anchor (an opening position taken up by one party from which they will move but such movement will come at a price). The aim of anchoring is to provide credibility to the extreme and yet realistic opening position, effectively setting an anchor. Movement becomes relative to the anchor. If you open with your position first and are able to get the other party talking about it, even if this means them rejecting it, it is your position which has becomes anchored in their mind. Unless they make a counter-offer. Often they become so preoccupied with attacking your position, they forget all about their own position.

***Sow the seed early*** *(Power required 4, Relationship erosion 3)*

This can take the form of the advance telephone call, which is designed to introduce an idea or a position, allowing for any emotional reaction to take place prior to the meeting. Or ideas that are introduced and parked in earlier meetings in the knowledge that they will need to be addressed in subsequent meetings. Sowing the seed early is based on getting inside their heads and adjusting their expectations.

***The power statement*** *(Power required 3, Relationship erosion 5)*

Opening statements are designed to manage the aspirations of the other party. They are usually used as a statement in the form of an assumed fact. The idea is to test an assumed position of power by effectively telling them that whilst you are in a position of "indifference," they are under pressure to conclude the deal with you: "I understand that you need an agreement in place by the end of the day," or "I want to make it clear that today's discussions are to ensure that we have given you every opportunity to win the business." The language is that used by a "Critical Parent" by implying assumed authority designed to get the other party talking and thinking about how they are going to move towards you.

***The mock shock*** *(Power required 8, Relationship erosion 6)*
This is an extension to the power statement where you start the meeting by implying that all is lost: "We have decided that given your current performance levels and clearly no desire to offer compensation, terminating the contract is the only option for us." Or, "This may only be a small order, but failure to agree could affect all of your business with us." The devastating consequences of non-cooperation can shock the other party into reconsidering their position or backtracking from the outset, where saving the relationship becomes their primary objective.

***The professional flinch*** *(Power required 1, Relationship erosion 2)*
This is a shock reaction to their opening position. Both physically whether by extreme facial reaction and/or verbally, you are demonstrating your shock and surprise at their position. Used regardless of their opening offer and designed to lower their aspirations, the professional flinch has the effect of undermining their confidence in their position and expectations.

***The broken record*** *(Power required 4, Relationship erosion 5)*
This is a tactic which involves them repeating their position. The more they repeat it, the more credible it becomes. The more their position is discussed, the more likely the discussion will revolve

around their position not yours. They start to sound like a broken record but the message gets through. Of course this can be interpreted as intransigence and can result in you losing patience and concluding the meeting. They will require a moderate amount of power of around 4/10 to be able to carry it off.

5. Empowerment

The fifth category of tactics involves the degree to which you are authorized to trade (see also Chapter 7), and the extent to which others need to be involved in the decision-making process.

***Higher authority*** *(Power required 1, Relationship erosion 5)*

The use of the boss or a mysterious and distant overseeing body required to sign off any movement, agreements, or individual issues beyond those limits that you are allowed to trade. The idea is to convince the other party to agree within the level you are authorized to go to, so that they can complete the deal today, rather than risk the deal being jeopardized, or so as not to allow your boss to see the other concessions that you have already offered. It's also used to disassociate yourself from not being able to accept a proposal: "That's out of my control and I will need to come back to you on that one."

***Defence in depth*** *(Power required 3, Relationship erosion 5)*

This is where several layers of decision-making authority allow for further conditions to be applied each time the agreement is referred. Typically it's where your customer states that they will take the deal for sign-off to their boss. A day later, the call comes that, subject to one final concession, the deal will be agreed. You reluctantly agree. A day later, your customer calls and states that their boss has signed it off and it's now been sent for approval to the board and that if you could just agree to the 30 days payment terms it will gain agreement. Reluctantly you agree and ask if they will let you know when it has been approved. The next day, your customer calls to again advise you that the board have now signed it off and they have now handed it over to Health and Safety for final approval and then advise you of yet another small concession that will be necessary if "final" sign-off is to be achieved. You should always understand the decision-making levels and process, otherwise you leave yourself exposed to defence in depth.

***Use of official authority*** *(Power required 1, Relationship erosion 4)*
This is used where one party disempowers themselves saying that they cannot or are not allowed to change the terms. They refer to their own company policy, legal requirements, association requirements or even historical precedents and, although sometimes true, it's often a tactic in play used to legitimize their position. "Our company policy is 60 days payment on all transactions and there is nothing we can do about that." It's frequently used to provide rationale in an attempt to bolster the credibility of their proposal. Ensure you insist that such constraints are their problem and one that you welcome suggestions on how they plan to work around them in order to avoid you having to escalate the issue.

***"It's all I can afford"*** *(Power required 1, Relationship erosion 2)*
This is used to suggest that budgets are finite, the specification is fixed and that it's all that is available: "I have no other funds available so take it or leave it." It's designed to place the onus of obligation on the other party, implying that they need to work within that which

you can afford. In contrast, when faced with such tactics the receiving party can change the specification, the volume, the timing or any variable that helps to naturalize the implications of the fixed fee.

***Onus transfer*** *(Power required 2, Relationship erosion 3)*
Transferring the obligation for suggestions and ideas onto the other party, to make it their problem. "We have a problem in making our payment on time this month. We can make the transfer but it is going to be five days late, how do you want to deal with this?" Once they have been advised, the problem becomes a shared one. The implications may still sit squarely with you but you have transferred the onus onto the other party.

***Off-limits*** *(Power required 3, Relationship erosion 2)*
Where issues are positioned as off-limits (non-negotiable or "off the agenda" for the purpose of these discussions). They are often described as "things I can't agree, so let's focus on the terms we can agree today." Remember, nothing is agreed until everything is agreed. Their motive is to protect some of the more critical issues from negotiation. This can also result in a negotiation over what is negotiable before the real negotiation even begins. This tactic is commonly used in political negotiations but regularly features in all types of commercial settlement negotiations too.

***New faces*** *(Power required 2, Relationship erosion 4)*
When a new person takes over the relationship or a new account manager is introduced, both past precedents and history carry far less relevance. New faces need not be tied to or constrained by what has happened in the past. They can sometimes offer a solution to

deadlock where personalities stand in the way of progress. They can provide for a fresh examination of affairs or can even be used to intimidate the other party where the seniority of the new negotiator carries certain gravitas. Retailers are renowned for changing their buyers systematically and periodically so that new faces remove the familiarity of an existing trading relationship. This keeps the focus on terms fresh and removes any scope for complacency.

### 6. Moving the costs around

The sixth category of tactics comes from reconfiguring the package or specification or manipulating the terms in order to provide a different complexion to the deal. The relationship between specification and price is used by many tactical negotiators as a means of manipulating the cost of supply, whilst attracting the best possible price.

***The building block technique*** *(Power required 3, Relationship erosion 5)*
This is where one party requests a price but only for part of their actual requirements. During your exploratory meeting, you then request prices for various quantity arrangements, ranging up to and including your actual needs. The idea is to manage expectations in the first instance and understand the relative cost/price differences and implications across the different arrangements. This can reveal much about their cost base and margin structure. You then negotiate for a one-year agreement for example, in the knowledge that you can raise this to a three-year agreement. You then seek incentives from the other party in the event that you could extend the agreement to two years, and then negotiate incremental terms for this "doubling" of the contract. Finally, you broaden the discussion to a

three-year partnership. Of course, to agree to such a deal, you will require more preferential terms.

The building block technique involves planning out your stages which can apply to any variable and provides time for the other party to adjust to concessions that would otherwise be difficult to extract.

***Wipe the proposal off the table without saying no*** *(Power required 3, Relationship erosion 2)*

Each time they make a proposal, you say "yes, subject to our terms." Your terms turn out to be either equally as outrageous, or are financially designed to offset the implications of agreeing to them. One party says: "Your discount levels based on last year's performance are being adjusted from 10% to 7.5% for the year ahead." And the other party responds: "Subject to you improving your promotional funding from $100,000 to $250,000 for the year, we will accept the reduction in discount."

The response from the first party will inevitably be: "We can't do that" to which you suggest: "and that's why we are not in a position to accept your position." You rarely need say no in a negotiation. Just find a way, a basis, a set of conditions upon which the consequences, be they financial, risk or third-party implications, are neutralized by the terms you attach to it.

***Linking the issues*** *(Power required 2, Relationship erosion 3)*

Everything is conditional and therefore linked to other conditions. Linking the relative values and importance of issues is key to ensuring that linked issues gain the attention you require. This is sometimes used to protect certain terms. For example, if the contract length was very important to one party and they knew that a high value variable to the other party was attracting a 10,000 volume order, the two would be linked to ensure that the contract length issues could not be easily dismissed.

***Side issue or red herring*** *(Power required 2, Relationship erosion 6)*
This is where some issues are introduced onto the agenda that have been positioned to lose or trade off against. Later during the negotiation, value is traded as each of the red herrings are conceded, having played their part in attracting improved terms elsewhere. For example, you need to attract shorter lead times and improved discounts. Both items are on the agenda as is a new termination clause, allowing you to terminate the contract with very short notice and lower volume discount thresholds. The last two are effectively red herrings which you expect to concede on. However, in doing so you are able to trade for better terms on lead times and discounts.

***The slice*** *(Power required 4, Relationship erosion 1)*
This is where you believe that the issue is of high value to the other party and trade against the issue in "slices." For example, you know that volume is critical to them. You are currently at 50,000 units and know that your requirement is for an order of 150,000 units. Rather than trade up to 150,000 units, you trade to 80,000 in return for a concession. Later you trade to 100,000 for a further concession, then to 115,000 and so on. Each move is conditional on a concession, ensuring that the value of your total move is maximized.

7. Deceit

There is no other way to describe the seventh and final category of tactics: deceit. If reputation or relationships hold any value to you or your business, think twice before using the following. More importantly, be wary of those who carry a different view and choose to use deceit – they may choose to use it on you even after the contract has been signed.

***Trojan Horse*** *(Power required 2, Relationship erosion 7)*
This is named after a tactic used during the ancient war on Troy, which led to the saying: "Beware of Greeks bearing gifts." The Greeks left a gift in the form of a wooden horse outside Troy. The Trojans accepted the gift and brought it inside Troy only to find once accepted that the horse was full of soldiers ready to invade. Beware if the deal is too good to be true. This relates to the hidden small print, and the conditions and issues which can literally come out of the woodwork after the deal has been completed. The Trojan Horse represents a package created to entice you. Once accepted, it has some surprises in store because much of the downside was hidden at the time of agreement.

***The incorrect summary*** *(Power required 2, Relationship erosion 7)*
Where one party summarizes from their perspective, leaving out or even adjusting some of the terms discussed earlier. The idea is that you won't notice or won't challenge through fear of jeopardizing progress. Try to ensure that you summarize progress throughout the meeting and that you do so from your perspective. Also, ensure that you summarize in writing after the meeting. If you don't agree on what you believe you have agreed, then you're unlikely to have an agreement which is going to stand the test of time.

***Deliberate misunderstanding*** *(Power required 2, Relationship erosion 8)*
So as to open up areas which have already been regarded as

concluded, one party introduces a condition which they know to be unacceptable. After you have responded with confusion or start to demand clarity they adopt an "innocent misunderstanding" stance. Their motives could be varied, but it is usually related to stalling progress or to allow them to try and renegotiate terms that have otherwise been regarded as closed.

***The dumb foreigner*** *(Power required 1, Relationship erosion 3)*
They choose not to understand you at a given time during the negotiation due to language difficulty. This is especially used once the subject of price is introduced. As they seek to take up a firm position, they appear increasingly confused by what you have to say as you attempt to explain your position. When faced with such behavior, patience, restating your position, and maybe even a "time-out" is needed to dampen their confidence.

***The loss leader*** *(Power required 3, Relationship erosion 3)*
I have listed the "loss leader" under deceit because it involves one party convincing the other to agree to a deal at highly preferential rates, which will lead to benefits in the future. These "benefits" are often not contractual, conditional, or delivered on. In fact they are often used as a precedent: "You were able to offer that price last time we worked with you so we know you can do it again." If you are to enter into such agreements always ensure that it is in writing and the conditions are clearly stated in the contract.

## CONCLUSION

Tactics are an innate part of negotiation. They are part of any negotiator's armory. The risk/benefit of making use of tactics is only something you can judge based on your own circumstances, motivation and values. If you are to make use of tactics it is also worth noting that more than one tactic will often be combined to greater effect as they may seek to manipulate the balance of power and use psychological pressure on you. For example, "good cop, bad cop" may be combined with "physically disturbing them"; the "slice" may be linked to "higher authority" in an effort to add weight to their proposal. We should maintain an awareness both of the nature of tactics used in meetings and also the implications of adopting them ourselves.

Where you are able to operate as a conscious competent negotiator, your increased awareness of the tactics or values in play by the other party will help you see before you what is and what they want you to believe. You will also be presented with the choice to deliberately use tactics yourself for short-term advantage or to neutralize the gamesmanship of others you negotiate with.

As our standard for negotiating unfolds we have grasped how the concept of capitalism impacts on negotiation via the clock face in Chapter 2, and how power featured in Chapter 3 affects the negotiation strategies available to us. We have explored those traits within us that serve to underpin our behaviors in Chapter 4 supported by the fourteen behaviors of the Complete Skilled Negotiator featured in Chapter 5. Chapter 6 examined the psychological emotion that will challenge us wherever perceived conflict exists; followed in Chapter 7 by how scope and pressure can be controlled via the use of empowerment. With a grasp of values and tactics we are now ready to apply ourselves and for this we need to conduct the most important of exercises: planning.

# CHAPTER 9

# Planning and Preparation that Helps You to Build Value

A negotiation standard could never be complete without providing for the most fundamental element of negotiating: planning and preparation. It is only when the deal is done that the value of planning can be fully appreciated. In all my experience I have concluded that there is a direct correlation between how well you have planned and the contribution that your performance can make to the outcome of your negotiations.

To start with it is important not to get confused between knowledge and *ability*. What you understand will help you to perform but it will still depend all your skills as a Complete Skilled Negotiator. As part of your planning, understanding how to calculate risk, build agendas, develop conditional proposals, and grasping the concept of relationships counts for nothing if you don't possess the motivation to *do* these things, and that requires making time to plan and prepare. Ignore or avoid this reality at your peril. There will be many reasons, excuses and time distractions, that may or may not be valid, that may impact on your performance as a negotiator. But without preparation before you enter the "negotiation arena," all the theory in the world (and indeed this book!) will add up to nothing.

In negotiation, you can optimize your performance if you are disciplined enough to plan and prepare. There is no easy way around this, although I have tried to make the process of tactical planning as simple as possible, but the benefits of this time invested are many. Planning provides the opportunity for you to take control and sometimes even create something from nothing.

### *Planning creative trade-offs which realize additional value*

**engineering value**
This is where you use all the variables at your disposal to maximize total potential value.

In Felix Dennis's book, *88 The Narrow Road,* he claims that there are six ways of obtaining capital: to inherit, win, steal, marry, earn or borrow it. Extending the notion of earning it, I would like to add another. It is called *negotiating* it – because in negotiation you can create capital through the way you **engineer value**; by constructing deals which both realize value, contain risk and maximize opportunity.

But first we need to take the time to bring the pieces of the deal together in the right order. It is the planning and preparation that provides us the space to think through and qualify what each of the variables available means. If you have ever played the game *Tetris* you will know there is a skill involved in getting the right shapes in the right places and in the right order to maximize your score. If you do not adjust the pieces or move the shapes as they become visible they will simply stack up on each other, leaving your with lots of gaps and a low score. Similarly, in negotiation and working with variables, there is a skill in agreeing to the way and order in which you position the variables. Your motivation and mindset, not to mention flexibility, in moving variables around, provides endless possibilities to maximize the value, all driven by your planning. In the negotiation, the value you create can depend on the degree to which you can shape each variable to minimize any gaps between you and the other party.

As a Complete Skilled Negotiator your planning and preparation will be influenced by the number of variables and therefore possibilities available. This proactive and open-minded approach will provide you with a fundamental advantage in working out what each aspect of the deal means to the other party. You would not try to build a house without having completed the drawings, worked through your calculations and estimated your costs. You would know instinctively that the project would most likely fail without a plan. Negotiation is no different because once you have started, you should seek to maintain a proactive position and remain in control. Without a plan, you are more likely to be in a reactive position exposing yourself to circumstances and a position which can easily spiral out of your control.

## EACH AND EVERY DEAL IS UNIQUE

It is the uniqueness of each deal that creates opportunity and the need to plan each time.

Every negotiation you enter will have a set of circumstances surrounding it that effectively make it unique, even those which exist in familiar relationships. Your relationship, timing, market changes, the options you may have, how important the agreement is, and the issues to be agreed, will between them provide for dynamics and options that will create a unique set of circumstances. Working out exactly what is it that is unique to each negotiation you face will also enable you to be creative in your planning. Recognizing this also helps you to get "inside the other person's head," work with a more complex mix of variables with clear financial values and tackle the more ambiguous or intangible variables which can often hold the key to additional value.

**CASE STUDY**

A negotiation between two companies which involved the supply and distribution of cardboard packaging across Europe started with an exploratory meeting during which it became apparent that 35% of the supplier's cost was associated with the distribution of the packaging to various manufacturing sites. Having understood this unique set of circumstances the buyer was able to arrange for backhauling distribution through their own business, reducing the distribution cost element by 80%. Needless to say, the buyer went on to trade the backhauling opportunity for a significant improvement in other terms. It was a classic case of one party making it their business to understand the other party's business, their costs and their processes and then use this information to trade other issues more effectively.

Even when you have invested in time preparing it's important to realize that, once discussions get under way, and because each deal will be different, you should expect the unexpected. New ideas, consequences and issues will surface during your meetings. These may come in the form of a proposal or a demand you may not have considered before and, being new, you will need to make time to think through the possible implications and of course your response. However, because an idea is new, don't reject it because you have yet to consider the implications or cannot calculate the risks immediately. Often there's a signal within the proposal which relates to what's important to them. New ideas can also help you to work out what is going on in the other party's head.

## UNDERSTANDING VALUE

There are five things which can happen to value in negotiation. You can:

1. give it
2. create it
3. share it
4. protect it
5. take it.

As part of your tactical planning you will have considered the clock face and decided on your strategy. If you are planning to increase prices and there are no trade-offs involved, unless your customer is passing the price increase directly on to their customer, they may regard the negotiation as you simply looking to "take" value especially if you impose your demand without offering anything in return. With enough power and at 4 o'clock, you have set out to take value which they in return will have to concede. However, before you can impose such a price increase you need to consider the balance of power. For example, the fact that you can tell your kids what to do doesn't mean that it will always be the best thing to do, as you consider the longer-term implications for your relationship. In other words, the more powerful you are the more options you have but you need to remain mindful of the longer-term dependency in play.

### *The three dynamics of value*

In negotiation, as in business, the general offer is that you can have "it" quick, good or cheap. Now pick any two.

In other words, if you are offered all three, you are likely to be getting something which is "too good to be true." "Quick" usually means now and for most suppliers it means additional cost. "Good" can mean high quality but will usually come at greater cost. "Cheap" may be possible but the quality may suffer and the speed may not be as quick as you need.

There are many things in life you can obtain quick and cheap. Take the hamburger: the quality is not going to be that of a prime steak despite what the marketing might suggest. You can get a great first-class airline seat immediately (good and quick) but it will cost you a fortune. You can get a beautiful garden if you plant and tend it yourself at a reasonable price, but it might take a year or two for the benefits to arrive. These three dynamics of value fit together in the same way as risk and benefit go hand in hand in that one will nearly always affect the other. For instance, if you want low risk you expect the cost to rise because low risk comes at a price. Similarly, if you are prepared to take greater risk you will probably be offered better returns.

### *What do we mean by total value?*

In most negotiations there is a central issue. This principle can relate to the price of an office lease, a trade union challenging changes to working practices, or an internal negotiation over who gets what percentage of the marketing budget. The fact that many negotiations have a central issue provides you with an opportunity to better negotiate around it by introducing and trading it against other related variables, considerations and implications, all of which will have some bearing on the total value.

**CASE STUDY**

A YouTube video clip that features a businessman on the phone, negotiating with his dentist for a tooth removal providing an excellent example of how to get the best price at any price. During the phone call he continuously stresses to the dentist that the cheapest price is all that's important to him. The businessman "negotiates" the price down by first agreeing not to have a supporting nurse, then any numbing jabs, and he continues to negotiate the price down till the dentist is literally agreeing to rip the tooth out. The patient is due to experience excruciating pain for the lowest price. The punchline comes when a price is agreed and the businessman agrees to send his wife around for the treatment that afternoon.

Of course we can all get a great price, but someone in your business, possibly you, could be facing the consequences of a de-specified product or service.

Try to remove *price* as the main issue of contention. It is the most transparent of issues ("what you get, I lose and what I get, you lose") and the most contentious of issues, especially when dealt with in isolation. Indeed, even if you negotiate creatively around a range of variables but leave price until the end you are likely to finish up back at 4 o'clock – hard bargaining. With nowhere to go you are just as likely to deadlock at the end over price as if price had been the only issue under consideration. So introduce it early on and link it to other conditions. Keep it in the mix, and conditional.

**hard bargaining**
This term is used to describe win–lose negotiations involving aggressive positioning, tough tactics which serve to exploit any weakness in the other party's position which are in your short-term favor.

By introducing it early you can always re visit it as part of changing other terms during the negotiation.

Total value comes not only from the basic terms agreed, but also from certainty on whether the deal will actually deliver the value intended over the lifetime of the agreement.

**CASE STUDY**

A terracotta manufacturing company based just outside Barcelona was involved in a negotiation with a hotel chain to supply 2000 large (1.5 metre tall) plant/tree pots. The buyers were keen to enter into a replenishment contract. They knew that 5–7% of the pots got broken around pool sides each year and were of course insured against accidents created by guests. However, they wanted to ensure that they could replenish exactly like for like within days of an accident taking place.

The terracotta company had not entertained the idea of "maintenance contracts" before, but soon started to understand the benefits of such an agreement. As the negotiation commenced, there was much discussion around price, delivery, lead times, breakages, payment terms and the other usual variables. The discussions were between the sales director, Carlos, and the hotel buyer, Rodrigo. Having prepared and conducted some calculations, Rodrigo placed a risk-based proposal before Carlos.

"If you supply us with replacements without charge for the next three years, limited to no more than 10% of those originally purchased, we will commit to an order of 2000 pots per year for the next three years to support our new hotel opening programme."

Carlos knew the cost of manufacturing the pots was 40% of that for which they were sold. He was operating on a 60% gross margin so the actual potential cost of accepting the offer was 4% in return for which he would receive a long-term agreement to supply identical pots, the value of which far exceeded the maximum 4% risk. They then went on to discuss a further 12 variables before finally agreeing. It was the initial exchange of risk which created the momentum for the agreement to come together. What felt like a win–win for both from the outset encouraged them to work on what turned out to be a strong and sustainable agreement.

They could have just haggled over the price, faced the consequence of poor service levels and out-of-stock pots when they needed replenishments, but both were prepared to entertain the bigger picture based on a partnership that improved the total value opportunity.

Where you are reliant on the other party's motivation to deliver over the lifetime of the agreement, to perform or comply, and in the event that their performance falters, you or your business will be exposed to the implications of such shortfalls. So part of your consideration needs to focus on the period of time known as "follow through." This means asking the question:

"What if they are not able to fulfil their obligations? How can we build in clauses or variables which recognize and address this risk as part of the original agreement?"

Not only should your terms set out to protect and ensure adequate compensation in the case of lack of compliance or performance, but your terms should also ensure that the consequences to your business are addressed and compensated for, removing the need for further negotiations.

## THE SIX PRIMARY VARIABLES

In most negotiations there are six primary variables that tend to feature, which can be used to broaden out the scope of the agreement. This helps to capture all the issues that are likely to affect the total value of your agreements. Once defined, you can then consider the consequences of performance around each of these variables. During your planning this also provides you with the opportunity to introduce a range of conditions linked to each variable. These six variables apply across any type of deal from business to politics:

1. **Price, fee or margin** (how much will be paid).
2. **Volume** (how many, how much, or what types).
3. **Delivery** (when, where, response times).
4. **Contract period** (when it will start, how long it will run for, under what circumstances it will or can be terminated, when it will be reviewed etc).
5. **Payment terms** (when, how, currency etc).
6. **Specification** (what the product, service or agreement will include, the quality or how it will be supported).

### 1. Price, fee or margin

You can also build agreements which feature differing pricing structures. These can be linked to issues such as:

- the purpose for which the product or service is to be used;
- geography (regional pricing to be used and by whom);
- relationship loyalty.

They should also be linked directly to the other five primary variables.

When you negotiate price without linking to other variables, the transparency involving "what I get you lose and what you get, I lose" will usually result in tough positional bargaining. So try wherever possible to link price with other issues.

### 2. Volume

There are few cases where volume does not feature in negotiations and in most cases there is a direct relationship between price and volume, unless you are buying a one-off event or specific tangible item. The economies of scale usually provide for this, so much so that some businesses will reflect such a relationship on a published discount tariff. As an extension to the price list, this is also designed in an attempt to preempt further negotiation. Volume thresholds can sometimes be linked to retrospective discounts (a discount you receive on the whole order, but only when a certain volume order has been achieved) or can provide increased discount levels, depending on volume levels to promote loyalty and volume orders.

### 3. Delivery

Delivery refers to where, by when and how, which not only relates to the physical product to be delivered, but can also relate to the services to be provided or completed within agreed timescales.

Where delivery is stipulated to be by the end of the month for example, further variables can be introduced aimed at stipulating the consequences the other party will face if delivery commitments are not met. This can take the form of a penalty clause, or other forms of compensation linked to protecting against implications in the event that commitments are not met.

The construction industry uses this approach on work completion where contractors have to finish within certain timelines in order to allow others to start work. If they do not, there are financial implications for both the main contractor and other sub-contractors. So the risk and consequences are negotiated into the agreement so that responsibility and implications around timescales sit with the sub-contractor. They in turn may choose to negotiate terms that accommodate shared risk, recognizing circumstances beyond their control like weather:

"If it rains for more than 50% of the days we have to complete the job, we will be allowed a further ten days to complete without penalty."

#### 4. Contract period

Think of the contract duration. The start, stop, pause, cancel, recommence terms, each with different circumstances attached, and you can start to imagine just how many variables could be included when you consider contract period. For those involved in negotiating lease contracts, this is one of the most valuable variables in that to attract a five-year agreement rather than a one-year agreement buys so much more security and certainty.

Even if it is a rolling contract (ongoing) there will still be circumstances upon which an opt-out clause can be contractually exercised. Another variable designed to protect contract period commitments is termination, where you stipulate where one party can terminate the contract with or without reason or consequence as well as defining when the option to renew becomes available.

### 5. Payment terms

There are so many ways of constructing payment terms to reflect the risk to those involved, the commitment to see the work through, or simply to increase the value of the deal. They can be broken down to include:

- when and how payment will be made;
- advanced deposits;
- phased payments;
- even circumstances where delayed payment may be acceptable;
- late payment penalties.

Proposals that include payment terms can be triggered based on performance, can be held on account, paid retrospectively, be refundable, or with a defined number of days credit.

Sometimes payment terms are a reflection of cash flow requirements, the risks associated with the creditworthiness or history of the other party or simply a reflection of the standard terms of the dominant party in the negotiation.

Whichever one of these feature, payment terms have a financial implication for both parties and will feature as a primary variable.

### 6. Specification

Specification relates to almost anything that affects the quality of the product or service being offered. As a simple illustration, the materials specification of a garment in addition to design can relate to size, fabric, wash type, buttons, zips, lining, finishing, presentation and packaging, and each of these will have a multitude of options each impacting on the cost or value of the finished product. Imagine the number of variables involved for a company sourcing aircraft from one of the main manufacturers with literally thousands of specifications which all affect the total outcome of the agreement. The complexity of the product or service, where it is being sourced from, the financing arrangements, and the relationships involved will all have some impact on the level of detail and the number of variables that will relate to specification.

## WORKING WITH VARIABLES

Whenever the focus and pressure is on price, there is a tendency for negotiators to renegotiate other variables as part of offsetting any implications on price movement. This usually involves introducing other variables as part of compensation for or adjusting the price point. By ensuring that the other five primary variables remain linked to any changes to price the Complete Skilled Negotiator can maintain the total value on offer despite price pressures. In other words, this is about moving the package around to attract protection or grow the total value. Everything is conditional – which allows you to protect the value – so if one variable needs adjusting down others should be moved to offset the implications.

## CASE STUDY

A marketing company called Zen were negotiating a contract with one of their clients. The contract involved the development of creative ideas, the execution of website content and the production of associated printed materials. Central to Zen's "standard conditions" was that it reserved all rights to all the materials created. In other words, the copyright was to remain theirs regardless of any other terms agreed. This was despite having been paid by the client to create original content. Meanwhile the client's "standard terms" specified that they would own all copyright on all the materials specifically created for the client.

The negotiation that followed involved breaking down and categorizing the different types of work involved. Much of the content was specific to the client and original, and some of the work was software-based and could potentially be used for other clients, providing Zen with a low cost solution to their other clients using multimedia video content via their websites. They eventually agreed to those areas which one party would own and those which the other party would own. If both parties had dug in to protect their "standard terms," it's likely they would have come to a deadlock. However, both parties were instead prepared to break down and repackage around the copyright issue. The dependency and motivation which existed between the two companies to find a solution prompted the flexibility which was enough to help them establish a workable solution.

The second example provides an illustration of how a restaurant manager managed to remove the impact of any price increases for the next two years through perseverance and some creativity.

## CASE STUDY

A restaurant chain was involved in reviewing its wine list and decided to invite two suppliers of champagne in to discuss terms. The preferred supplier had supplied a range of four champagnes for the past six years and had so far refused to budge on its 5% annual price increase. The restaurant owner had lined up a BATNA (Best Alternative to a Negotiated Agreement ) with another supplier who could provide an equally good range and choice. This alternative was marginally better in price terms, but he was not totally convinced about their "returns policy," which had always been acceptable with the existing supplier.

The restaurant owner summarized with his existing supplier once more:

"So you are happy with the contract to supply, but would prefer a longer contract and the opportunity to extend your range to include the Vintage Rosé retailing at $90 a bottle."

He went on: "If you maintain last year's pricing for the duration of the contract, I will list the Rosé and extend our commitment to a two-year deal."

The sales manager quickly rejected the offer, stating the price increase agreement in place was non-negotiable. The restaurant was buying 500 bottles a year so the restaurant manager took a different angle.

"If you provide me with 25 bottles of the Rosé on a complimentary basis to help with the launch of the product, I will agree to the price increase."

The sales manager looked interested because stock was an area where he had some flexibility and he was heavily incentivized to gain listings of the new Rosé. He countered with:

"I will provide the 25 bottles subject to an order for 100 bottles of Rosé in advance."

The restaurant manager repackaged one more time in a final attempt to make the deal work:

"Subject to volumes exceeding 500 bottles this year, there will be no annual price increase next year."

It was enough to clinch the deal and on terms that included an up-front incentive, better managed inventory and certainty around future pricing.

## KNOWING WHAT VARIABLES YOU HAVE TO WORK WITH

Planning and preparation consists of effort and investment of time that goes into creating something of value from the various components that, when put together, lead to more value than the sum total of the parts. What does aircraft construction or a work of art have in common with negotiation? Both have a need for planning, preparation and design.

However, it's easier to visualize the need to plan when creating something with a physical form compared with planning simply to build an agreement. You can more easily imagine the design and planning needed when creating a new aircraft, critical to it ever coming together let alone flying, in the first place. The creativity employed by an artist, starting with a blank canvas and with all the work to do ahead of them, requires flexibility and a mental picture for what will be. In both cases, options and creativity play a significant part in ensuring a successful outcome, as well as necessity for some visionary thought.

As a negotiator, planning starts with working across the relevant variables and linking the terms associated with them together in such a way so as to realize incremental value. Design and structure is similar in so many ways across disciplines and yet, because of the time pressures in negotiation, the potential consequences and dilemmas, the discipline of planning can easily escape us, resulting in ideas and possibilities not being considered and deals which are suboptimized, or worse still, may not even prove possible. During the planning phase, scoping and taking the opportunity to create value starts off with understanding the options and bringing together component parts or variables that will make the deal both possible and ultimately more valuable.

As a creative negotiator you can identify ways to exploit synergies within the deal and within the relationships involved, firstly

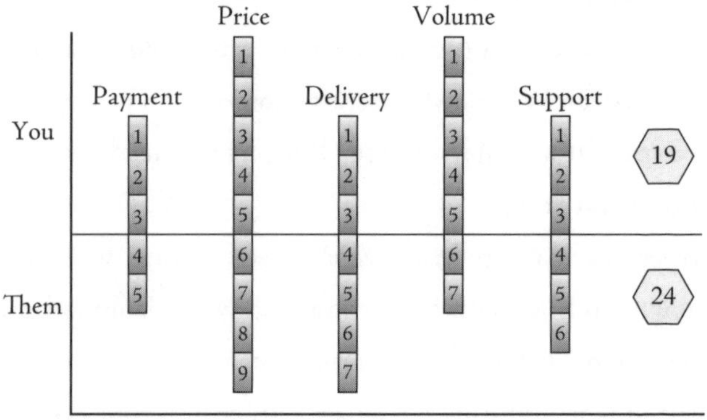


**Figure 9.1** Trading off variables.

by understanding as much about the deal from the other party's perspective. The process of exploration meetings to quality your preparation and any assumptions is one way of building a better understanding of how the deal might come together. This could be at a macro level where one business buys another to take advantage of cost saving, or build on market scale opportunities. Or it may be at a micro level, where each time you trade low-cost, high-value items in return for each other you effectively reduce costs, gain efficiencies or improve your terms.

Moving conditional proposals or variables around, changing who takes responsibility for what, shifting performance triggers, discount thresholds, performance conditions and contract terms in your negotiations is essentially about you establishing the point where both parties will agree. At the same time it is about how you can create more value as a result of how the deal has been put together. The more considered and structured you are in your approach to this, the more likely you are to negotiate a favorable agreement.

### *Attaching triggers to variables*

Most variables can be used on a sliding scale. For example, if you are discussing volume, the order could be anything from 1 to 1 trillion which of course would affect other variables.

However, volume can be linked to a trigger which sets off other terms you agree. For example, once you have ordered 1000 the 5% discount commences, or if you are able to place an order for 10,000 in any given month the delivery becomes free or, by agreeing to the total order now, we will allow you to draw off stock as you require it over the next six months. Each condition serves as a trigger which if met provides for the benefit offered.

Triggers can be applied to any variable and serve to motivate the behaviors of the other party as well as protect your interests. Variables can also have triggers attached to them which relate to a particular performance, beyond which or up to which another condition is met. For example, a discount that kicks in after the order for the first 200 has been received. The 200th order represents the trigger for the discount to become applicable. The payment terms can only be offered following receipt of the 20% deposit. Receipt of the full deposit is the trigger for the payment terms to be applicable. Terms are linked to a performance threshold (an order of 200), where further commitments then become applicable.

Once you have commenced your negotiation, you can trade off variables gradually, use absolute triggers and adapt trigger thresholds (performance levels) depending on what you want to achieve. With any variable, you can:

- adjust it;
- link it;
- place a trigger on it;
- or even move it bit by bit.

**the "salami" tactic**
Negotiating each variable slice by slice and each time attracting a benefit in return.

This is commonly known as **the "salami" tactic.**

As an example of trading off a variable gradually, you could link a quicker guaranteed response on the service provided conditional of a reduction in payment terms from 45 days to 40 days. You may trade a commitment to flexible delivery timings on spare parts in return for a further move to payment terms to 36 days. Perhaps you have the knowledge that they are really keen to get their 30 days payment agreed, which is their "symbol of success." So you go back and finally offer them the 30 days in return for a shorter termination notice period. Each time, you are attracting more value (or less risk by your calculation) than the very 15 days payment terms which you expected to move to in the first place. By this time, you may have calculated that although the 15 days have cost you the equivalent of 0.5% on the deal, the concessions you have attracted are worth 1.1%.

## RISK AS A NEGOTIABLE

The rate of change in business results in uncertainty in that even if a partnership relationship existed, based on an aligned strategy, how do you reasonably ensure that you remain continuously aligned as both your companies continue to reassess their strategies?

In other words, when considering the future and the contract you are about to sign, never assume a constant state. Things will always change over time. Performance, reliability, the market and the consumer can and usually do change, and should challenge your assumptions about how profitable the deal is, or will be, or has been.

It is these very issues driven by change which you need to factor into your planning, and your attitude towards accounting for these risks can often provide a means of attracting more valuable and more robust agreements. The concept of getting a great price but a lousy deal comes from an agreement where the price is good but the conditions or exposure you have accepted is so wide open, that it was worth the other party providing you with the better price given the security it had brought them.

The value to you of a guarantee which protects you against change, the value of accountability and responsibility are often not the same as the cost of accepting them.

In a similar way, the price or value of a flexible airline ticket will mean different things to you and the airline in the transaction; for example, the convenience of being able to switch and change can provide tremendous value to you. Imagine if you are having difficulty getting home from a business meeting late on a Friday night following a flight cancellation. Yet the absolute cost to the airline of offering a flexible service in many cases is negligible. So how much is this protection against change or the cost of inconvenience following change worth to you? Again, that depends on your circumstances.

Creative negotiators understand how to use convenience, flexibility and choice to build even greater levels of "total value" into their agreements from inside the head of the other party.

Where it is difficult to estimate or agree on risk, insurance also plays its part as a variable in negotiation. By insuring yourself or the other party against certain risks or insisting that they take out policies to protect against risks you can overcome some of the more challenging aspects of uncertainty.

You may not think twice about insuring your own contents in your house because of the known risks, or insuring your house from damage as for many it is their greatest asset. Equally, many people insure their health, their car (because the law says they have to), even their washing machine, just in case it stops working. Insuring against the possible and some cases probable is a further variable which can be used for accounting for risks. This same thought process is used as part of a negotiator's thinking as they identify ways of agreeing to terms whilst balancing the risks involved.

"In the event that you fail to meet the payment schedule, we reserve the right to reclaim the stock, or we will insure you against non payment." The premium will be built into the overall pricing structure. Either way you mitigate against the risk which is agreed as part of the negotiation based on the level of risk you see in play.

### *Protecting the value*

This involves protecting the value you think you have created in your agreement. What if delivery, specification or payment terms are not adhered to? What are the implications to you and how do you protect against them within the terms agreed? Negotiating risk firstly involves identifying the risks which could prevent the contract delivering what it's supposed to, and ensuring that the terms of the agreement reflect those risks to both parties.

In the same way that you have an interest in looking after your waiter at a restaurant, (assuming you do not want your meal to be tampered with!), you want to feel that your business partner is incentivized as far as possible on the same things as you are. Risks come in many forms and are often overlooked, as they do not necessarily reflect immediately on the Profit and Loss sheet. Ask any bank selling mortgages between 2004 and 2009. Ignore risk at your peril. Better still, trade it creatively against each of the primary variables. Insurance companies treat risk as a defined tangible issue and so should those of us buying or selling tangible products or services.

### *Accountability*

Once risks are identified, you can focus on who will take, insure, mitigate against or accept liability for the risks. Your next step involves building into your proposals a basis upon which the risks will be accommodated or compensated for. One challenge or opportunity – depending on how you see it – comes from understanding both parties' attitude to risk. If you have had a particularly bad experience in the past and the cost of putting it right still resonates, your attitude towards protecting against it and the value you associate with such cover may be greater than the cost implications for the other party providing it.

The guarantees provided with a second-hand car bought from a main dealer will have some value for which we accept that there will be a premium built into the price compared with buying privately. Many will regard this premium as a price worth paying. They are buying out the risk, buying confidence in that what they are paying is the maximum total price following any issues they may have with the car over the guaranteed period. They are buying certainty and for that they are prepared to pay. The way each party interprets the level of risk or even severity of that risk often varies based on their own circumstances and those individuals involved in the decision making on their behalf.

### *Risk is different for different people*

In the same way that supply and demand, and time and circumstances serve to set the balance of power in negotiations, risk and reward provide us with the basis for weighing up investment opportunities. Different industries have different tools for assessing risk and placing a premium on it, to hedge against it or insure against it. In some cases where the deal is of strategic importance they may even be prepared to accept some degree of uncertainty. Dealing with uncertainty over the long term may represent a good bet given the potential value at stake. Risk as a variable is not bad or to be avoided, it just needs to be recognized, understood and managed. Whether you are a private equity firm buying into a business, negotiating for mining rights, or buying computer chips from Korea, risk will feature in your considerations and the terms you agree.

In the field of litigation, for example, how do you place a cost or value on the risk or benefit of negotiating an out-of-court settlement? How does a PR company view the implications of risk associated with bad PR exposure and the degree to which this could affect their reputation versus the legal costs of defending one's reputation? It is probably too late to insure against such risks so you need to remain as objective as possible, set your break points and get inside the other party's head. Each case will be unique and can only be assessed by those facing the consequences.

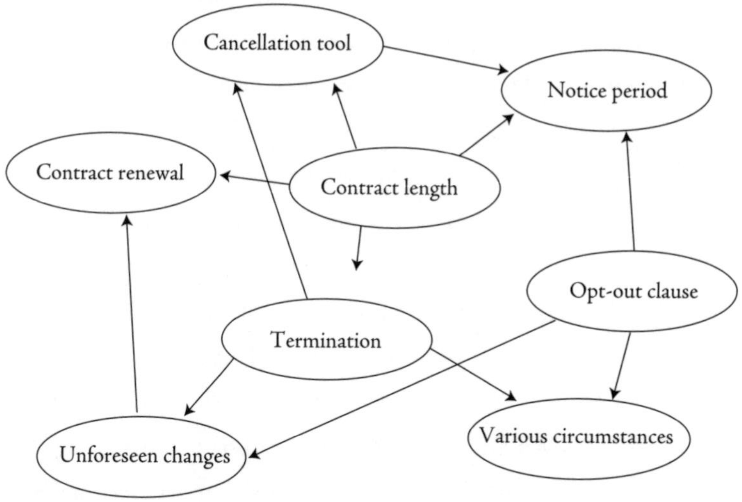


**Figure 9.2** Visualizing risk, relating to contract length.

## CASE STUDY

Imagine you are a buying manager involved in sourcing a particular fashion garment featuring the latest pop craze. You agree to increase your minimum volume order in return for a higher discount. However, in doing so you manage to overlook the warehousing implications, the impact of residual stock, and even the degree to which the garment may still be in fashion in three months. Each of these implications and others has to be considered if you are to manage the risks involved in placing the order, otherwise by simply negotiating to get the best price you are likely to finish up with a poor total value agreement.

## CASE STUDY

A travel insurance advert published in the press in 2010 provided a classic example of how variables can be linked together with conditions that manage the risks associated with the policy. The advert read as follows:

- "The insurance provides protection for an unlimited number of trips (providing that no trip is longer than 30 days, water sport for 17 days in any one year)
- "Worldwide cover is available to all (except for those aged over 70)
- "It's available for $10 a month (for the first 3 months, then $20 a month subject to a 12 month minimum contract)."

Every offer had a condition which either limited the risk to the insurer or reduced the absolute cost of offering the service in the first place. What made this example so obvious was that the conditions were not even hidden in the small print. This was the advert itself.

*Managing compliance and performance?*

If you missed your mortgage payment this month, your lender would want the outstanding payment at the earliest moment. They would also insist on charging further interest on the late payment. This same philosophy or considerations should exist with any agreement where risks are to be addressed. Without this consideration you may well find yourself involved with relationship issues through a lack of clarity around obligations where commitments are not met.

A useful way of exploring risk is to ask the question "What would happen if …?"

- They do not meet their deadlines?
- The specification falls short?
- They want to terminate early?
- Their circumstances change?
- Our circumstances change and we need more flexibility?
- Exchange rates fluctuate wildly?
- Their key personnel leave?

And so on. There are so many possibilities relating to the potential for change which many businesses are renowned for building into their "standard terms" in the small print. The reality is that these risks are two-way and wherever possible you should include them as part of your negotiation agenda.

## PREPARING TO MANAGE COMPLEXITY

How do we map the multiple variables in negotiations when planning? Negotiation in multi-issue deals involves packaging and repackaging variables together. It involves linking conditions and changing the terms that relate to each variable and to the interests, priorities and needs of the other party.

The shape of most deals, where a range of issues are involved, changes each time a new proposal is tabled. Changes in terms of total value happen throughout the negotiation until both parties agree to settle with a particular set of terms and conditions. The process provides a fluid situation, like watching shifting sands. The shape may get bigger or smaller, longer or shorter, fatter or thinner. This can make tracking the deal and the implications of changes difficult, and for this the Complete Skilled Negotiator uses a "Record of Offers" tool (page 299).

Building an agreement that entails a process involving many proposals is challenging because of the need to trade around specific variables whilst remaining mindful of the overall picture and total value implications.

For example, whilst negotiating an agreement which involves agreeing to guarantee that a job will be finished by the end of the month you may want to consider the things which you cannot control, like circumstances that might make the commitment difficult to meet. These could be categorized by both parties as valid reasons for the job being delayed.

### *Exploring all possibilities*

Other issues that will need resolving during your negotiations could also come at a price so the concept of "nothing is agreed until everything is agreed" allows you to carefully explore all possibilities and agree in principle to ideas subject to all other conditions being agreeable. If necessary you can take proposals back off the table in the event that conditions discussed latterly are not agreed or the overall deal becomes unacceptable. One danger to watch for as you explore possibilities is sending the other party signals regarding which issues you are prepared to agree to, or those which are of particular importance to you. It's OK to say yes to proposals in principle providing the other party is aware that any one proposal is subject to all other conditions being acceptable. With some trust, and the appropriate climate, the shape of the deal should be allowed to change and evolve. Most of the issues will be in some way interrelated because most will impact on the total cost or value.

I have heard of more challenging negotiations being compared with the building of a 10,000 piece jigsaw. First you group pieces together, perhaps edges, then gather the pieces into color zones. Then you start to piece together sections of the picture, leaving some pieces not fitting so you go off in search for the right piece so that you can continue. You need patience, persistence and an eye for how the picture is coming together. You know you have enough pieces, it's just a matter of the order, sequence and matching that's needed. With a jigsaw you have a picture forming, providing instant feedback on your progress. In negotiation you only have the response of the other party to rely on, but the way you approach the task has many similarities. With a jigsaw, however, the next piece may or may not fit. In negotiation a proposal that was rejected earlier may be accepted later under different circumstances. With a jigsaw you know it's possible from the outset as you have the right number of pieces to start with and to finish the task. In negotiation there is no such certainty and with a jigsaw there is one outcome that is as predicable as the picture is on the box. In negotiation, the shape of the deal can and usually does vary depending on how the negotiators have responded to each other's ideas and positions.

## THE NEED FOR AN OPEN MIND

You could argue that any concession asked for is acceptable, providing a reciprocal move is made to balance out the implications. For example, even a price increase might be acceptable, providing costs are being taken out, or performance is being enhanced in other areas, thereby neutralizing the effect. However, one should always be mindful of precedents that are being set and how they may affect other or later discussions. The creative negotiator can approach the deal understanding that anything is possible, as long as you can find a basis upon which it can be acceptable. If you can establish the issues which are important to both parties (the terms of which are not often the same) you can start to develop the necessary shape of the deal for it to become mutually acceptable.

Recognizing that there are many ways of achieving the same end helps to keep our minds open towards new opportunities. However, there is a skill involved in remaining balanced and focused on your own strategy and that of total value even when allowing new ideas onto the negotiation table.

### *Taking your time and being patient*

Working on the deal does not mean that each proposal should be met with approval, rejection or even a counter proposal. Some ideas need more work and time to consider before you can even respond to them. In most cases you can park issues, say payment terms and contract length, and continue to work through other parts of the agreement, say volume, discounts and ordering processes subject, of course, to the remaining items being agreeable. Be prepared to park issues which you can come back to later.

Where the number of variables makes the negotiation complex, you should (subject to time constraints) take the time to adjourn and consider the possibilities. When you are in need of further authorization or stakeholder buy-in, take the time to consult before responding. This is especially the case if your ideas are new or include less tangible issues such as flexibility, convenience or risk.

### *Being open to new ideas*

Flexibility not only increases the chances of your performance being more productive, but will also throw up new ideas for consideration that you might otherwise have filtered out very early on through being too single-minded or focused.

- If sustainable profit growth is the endgame, then allow yourself to explore how this can come about and make the time to do this.
- If you are involved in a conflict resolution negotiation, there may be a range of options available to you which achieve the same end, each with its own merits.
- If agreement to a "change in working practices" with the trade unions is what you are faced with, there will be a range of options available, each of which may facilitate an acceptance of change.

There is often more than one way to achieve your end result so try to remain focused on building solutions even where there is ambiguity or irrational behavior in play. The next time you feel the need for a quick resolution and find yourself considering compromises, ask yourself: "Am I buying myself certainty in obtaining an early commitment and effectively buying myself some "comfort," or should I make more time and be patient with the process?"

### *Agreeing in principle*

Throughout your discussions you've agreed to nothing until the end. Of course this could result in you sending the wrong messages and signals if you appear too open to ideas which are clearly not acceptable. Your attitude and response should remain balanced and, where necessary, point out how challenging some areas will be to entertain. Slow down and provide yourself time to think things through. Examine the "what ifs" and adopt a mindset of "how" and "under what circumstances," rather than "no," "can't" or "won't," which are so easy to adopt when you can't see the total picture.

### *Changing the shape of the deal – repackaging*

Creative negotiators avoid deadlock by identifying ways of changing the shape of the deal, which allows the other party to move. They do this whilst, at the same time, moving the value of the deal forward for themselves. The more you understand about the other party's position and points of interest, the more obvious this becomes.

Try to focus on what you can do, move your instinctive attitude from blame or defend to qualify, and then build solution-based proposals. Problem solving is far more rewarding and sustainable than seeking simply to drive down their terms.

### CASE STUDY

A marketing manager was planning to place an order with a printer for 20,000 brochures that needed to be delivered within 14 days, when their promotion was due to start. The brochures were to help support a weekend promotional offer, beyond which they become worthless, so timing on delivery was critical. The price, payment terms and specification had been agreed. The printer then agreed on the delivery date which was within 14 days. Payment would not be made until delivery had been received and no payment would be made if the 14-day deadline was not met. Although this gave the marketing manager some assurance that delivery would be made on time it did not guarantee it and this promotion was critical. The marketing manager restated the criticality of the timing and that if the brochures were late for any reason, they would be of no use. The printing salesman then quickly stated that he could not absolutely guarantee the date. The marketing manager paused and then responded with: "What do we need to do to ensure that without any risk they will be on time?" The salesman replied: "We could hire a van of our own and deliver direct, but that would increase the cost by $500." The value of the order was for $20,000. The marketing manager indicated that if the printer was able to provide this service at no cost, he would sign off the order.

The printer then responded with an idea:

"If we deliver to our local depot, which is only two miles from your offices, do you have the means to collect them overnight?"

The marketing manager responded with: "If you can deliver them within 12 days, I can arrange that," at which point they agreed on the deal.

Their problem-solving approach removed the potential for deadlock or incremental cost, resulting in two motivated business partners working together.

## PLANNING FROM A PRACTICAL PERSPECTIVE

I have saved what is probably the most important element of negotiation till the end. It is then both easy to find as a reference and to share with others. If preparation is critical to negotiation then preparing in a team, as a team, using the same thinking, language and approach is just as important as the act itself (see Chapter 7, page 211, "Negotiation using empowerment within team roles").

This approach, consisting of a number of tools, provides a standard for preparation which is easy to utilize and delivers consistency, confidence and certainty. It also ensures that you are thinking from inside the head of the other party in the way you evaluate the importance and value of variables and build an agenda aimed at maximizing value. The beauty of the planning process is that you can start with your primary variables, of price, volume, timescales and contract length, specification and payment terms. Your planning can then move on to examining the hidden costs. Planning and preparation provides the opportunity to work out the other party's costs and the values they will place on each variable.

The way variables influence total value agreements will differ for all parties involved. Some of the things which you regard as important or valuable may well be ranked differently from the value others place on them. Some of this will have been objectively assessed and some will be because you have been effective in preconditioning them around those variables with which you have some flexibility and those which are going to require some radical if not large concessions if you are to consider movement.

Options, possibilities and scoping value are more easily defined when you have the time and space to think clearly, involve others and weigh up your considerations, possibilities and risks objectively. Your first challenge is the discipline required to make the time and use it productively to plan through your negotiation. Some lack the belief that preparation will really pay off. (Those in denial who think they understand their market and can perform equally as well without preparation clearly have an ego issue!) Another challenge could be that in the past there has been a lack of a clear or respected process that has proved to deliver results, which can also dampen motivation. There are always other "things" you could be doing with your time but rarely one that will provide you with such certainty, alignment and confidence for your negotiation as a well-thought-through plan.

Exploring possibilities and potential variables allows you to consider how the other party view or value such issues. Planning is by its nature proactive and where you make the time to work through the possibilities you have already gained an advantage before entering the negotiating room. It's you who must drive the options, the agenda and the process, rather than being exposed to market forces and potentially becoming a victim of time, circumstances or supply and demand pressures which will be placed on you.

### *The process*

The first step in the planning process is commonly known as brainstorming; we call it trade-storming (page 291). It is the starting point from where you may want to involve other stakeholders to pool ideas or to challenge any assumptions.

It's surprising how often others will identify the risks that you might otherwise overlook because of your involvement with detail or because of your limited exposure to consequences.

To help simplify the scoping and planning process we have created a number of basic pro formas which fit logically together and have been used by hundreds of businesses globally for their negotiation planning.

| Tool | Purpose |
|---|---|
| Trade-storming (honeycomb) ↓ | Helps you to brainstorm potential issues |
| Trade surveyor ↓ | Helps you to prioritize low-cost/high-value trades |
| Issue map ↓ | Helps you to link and group relationships between tradable issues |
| Agenda* ↓ | Helps you to structure and gain clarity before and during the negotiation |
| Move planner* ↓ | Helps you to define initial specific conditional details |
| Record of offers* | Helps you to record and track proposals throughout the negotiation process |

*Operational tools used during the negotiation

**Figure 9.3** Planning tools.

The aim of the negotiation planning tools is to help you scope the potential of your deal, work out the relative values, plan out your initial proposals and then monitor the value of your agreement as discussions unfold.

### *Trade-storming*

The trade-storming tool is represented by a simple honeycomb model. It invites you to list each of the issues which you believe will feature as part of your pending negotiation, and then start to identify potential connections or relationships between them. The list is taken from your agenda. Trade-storming is effectively the same as brainstorming and can often help you to identify additional variables linked to the six primary variables. These are not always obvious to start with, which is why this tool is useful in helping you to visualize as you think through and expand on the more obvious variables. The Complete Skilled Negotiator will develop

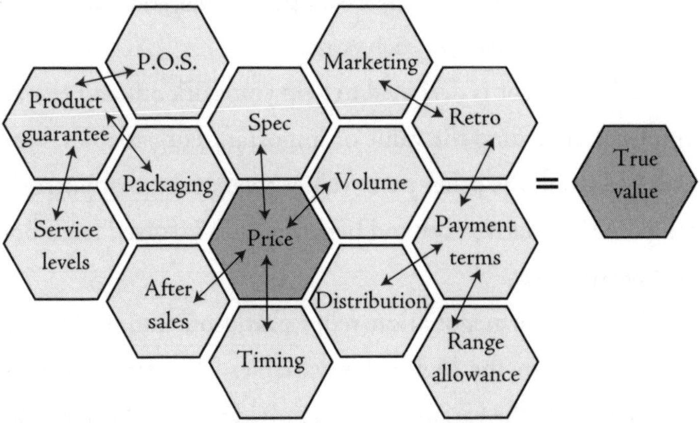


**Figure 9.4** Trade-storming.

several variables using the trade-storming tool as they consider how each variable can become linked or grouped by association with other variables. Delivery may be one variable but when you start to consider the issues which sit around delivery which are worthy of negotiation you could list timing, venues, response times, accuracy, regularity and so on. All will have some bearing on the value or cost associated with this element of the agreement.

### *Trade surveyor*

Ultimately you will need to form some initial conditional proposals for your meeting. Having worked through the variables most likely to feature on your agenda, your next job is then to work out the relative values involved for you and the other party.

This means categorizing each variable according to the interests, priorities and values the other party place on them. For this we use a pro forma known as a trade surveyor. It's useful to use this as part of your exploration meetings with the other party. During the discussions, you can qualify any assumptions that you may have on the value that they place on each issue.

The trade surveyor is designed to help you work out and test any assumptions regarding the value or importance of variables, based on how you think the other party values them. It is an opportunity to compare the relative cost and benefit values involved from both parties' perspectives.

Building value in negotiation relies partly on trading low-cost variables in return for high-value variables. The trade surveyor helps you identify the variables which provide you (or both parties) with an incremental gain. This approach provides a useful way of understanding the most likely value relationships in play and should

| Issues | Take | | Give | |
|---|---|---|---|---|
| | Value to us | Cost to them | Cost to us | Value to them |
| Price | High | High | High | High |
| Volume discount | | | Medium | High |
| Promotion fees | | | Low | High |
| Payment terms | | | Low | High |
| Distribution | High | Low | | |
| Volumes | High | Low | | |
| Promotions | High | Low | | |
| Exclusivity | | | Low | High |

Rate: High/Medium/Low For the purpose of examining possibilities

**Figure 9.5** Trade surveyor.

help inform you when developing conditional proposals prior to your meeting. Because of a lack of transparency, win–win usually means that one party wins (gains more value), but that the other party wins more. In other words, it's not about the fair, equitable 50–50 sharing of value as the term win–win might suggest. It is simply a process which attracts the interests of both parties because of the potential benefits available however this might be split; and conditional trading is central to this.

### *Issue map*

We use the issue map to visually work through the relative low-cost, high-value relationships and examine the different ways in which any one variable can be coupled with others, as part of building initial, conditional proposals.

Depending on the relative values you place on each variable, you can use the issue map to explore possible linkages. You may link

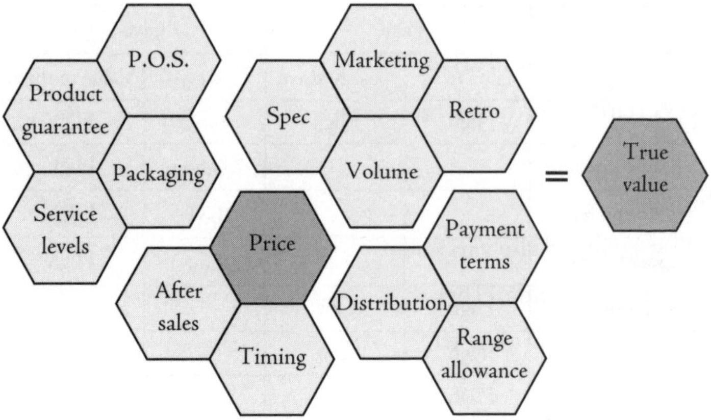


**Figure 9.6** Issue map.

price to volume or payment terms to delivery scheduling and so on. This is only a basic way of playing with possibilities but it allows you to consider different options before constructing specific proposals.

On your issue map you may, for example:

- draw a line for your own reference to indicate a potential coupling between price and volume;
- draw a line to couple price and specification as you weigh up the best way of linking issues.

Using your trade surveyor, you can start to draw potential links between each of the variables. You can start to visualize how they may be coupled for the purpose of constructing proposals. An obvious example is where volume and discount work together or where contract length and retrospective discounts are linked, and so on. You may even decide to table the three together, for example: "If you can offer a price of $300 a unit, we will place an initial order for 5000 units. This is subject to you manufacturing to our specification and of course, subject to all other terms and conditions being acceptable." Always remember that nothing is agreed until everything is agreed.

### *Agenda*

Having qualified the variables, it's time to pull together and communicate an agenda. This should preferably be one that you can both agree on and that will provide the basis and parameters for discussions.

The one benefit of a qualified agenda is that you know what has been tabled and what is outstanding. If you have worked through the timescales, costings and quality but know from the agenda that contract length and payment terms are outstanding issues, you still have plenty of scope to negotiate even if that means bringing timescales back on to the table by linking them to contract length. You

Agenda

1. Service and quality specification
2. Information and data sharing
3. Volume ordering
4. Fee structure
5. Discount levels
6. Commencement date
7. Contract period
8. Payment terms
9. Confidentiality

**Figure 9.7** Sample agenda.

can address unacceptable terms by linking them to proposals that are yet to be tabled. It can feel very open-ended at first, but by leaving flexibility around some of the issues as discussions evolve, you can discuss more openly and, depending on the level of trust, explore different options. Of course, there will be tension and positions in play which you will need to manage, so just remember to ensure your position at any point in time is conditional and clearly linked.

A mutually agreed agenda to work from can help you to manage some initial ambiguity and will help build trust. Agreeing to issues subject to all other issues being agreeable is all part of allowing the deal to take shape in the knowledge that you can always come back and revisit what you have notionally agreed if other issues prove too challenging. A comprehensive agenda provides a list of those issues which need to be agreed, giving everyone involved transparency. The idea of agreeing to one issue without everything else being lined up can feel exposing, and is the one area of ambiguity that you will have to accommodate.

### *The move planner*

The move planner is used to detail the specific conditional terms against each of the trade-offs you plan to make, providing you with a list of well-thought-through proposals.

Each proposal needs to be specific, allowing the other party the chance to calculate, weigh, consider and respond. It is no help to the negotiation process to simply plan to ask for improved payment terms in return for a higher volume order. You have to be more specific. If not, you can't reasonably expect them to take the offer seriously or be able to respond to it. If it's 60 days for a 10% increase, say so. Detail it on your move planner. It is the one place to record

Move Planner

| If you... | Then we... |
| --- | --- |
| Distribution 500 | Price £14.90 |
| Volume 1m | Volume discount 1.5% |
| Volume 1.3m<br>Promotions 6 | Marketing investment £80k |

**Figure 9.8** Move planner.

your proposals in advance of discussions. They are the conditions which you have thought through, calculated and have considered objectively in the cold light of day.

Before you start to make any proposals, qualify their priorities one last time. It is amazing how these can change over relatively short periods of time.

"Last week you told me that delivery by week 12 would work for you, now you are saying week 8. Just how important is week 8?"

Understanding how they value things right now is critical. I have seen people in negotiations trying to negotiate for what they think they want, rather than for what they actually need. Your questioning should be aimed at qualifying what they *need*.

Imagine a construction manager who insists on the scaffolding being removed from the construction site with one day's notice. He regards it as critical. The hire company is able to accommodate the request but will charge a premium for a quick response. When the builder is questioned, it comes to light that his construction contract states that he has seven days to clear the site. Seven days' notice will save him a 5% premium on the scaffold rental. It's not dissimilar to price. Most people think they want a better price but often it's a better deal or enhanced value that they really seek.

When tabling a conditional proposal, at first try to avoid introducing more than three items at once. It can prove difficult for the other party to calculate or respond to the proposal in any meaningful way. It also slows down any momentum created. If you table every conditional proposal you have prepared all at once, you are more likely to draw a blank or delayed response from the other party for three reasons.

1. They will find it incredibly difficult under pressure to calculate what it all means. Therefore, they are likely to only pick off the terms they do like, whilst ignoring the conditions attached to them.
2. They are left with the task of working out links or connections between each conditional proposal, which will potentially confuse them further still.
3. They will have some ideas which you might want to weigh up before tabling your entire position.

This approach of gradually tabling your proposals and allowing the deal to build requires patience and a certain degree of comfort with early ambiguity.

To start with, neither party will be able to see the whole deal and yet may be asked to respond to part of it. Remember, where there is complexity, you may need to park elements and come back to them later, having examined some of the other agenda points first.

### *The record of offers*

This is especially important when you are dealing with many variables and you need to maintain a clear record of progress. Negotiators are often found scribbling notes in no particular order, as the deal unfolds. Before long, you can barely make sense of the notes, or what the other party has suggested, let alone the last full position tabled. The "record of offers" table allows you to record all positions and movement, enabling you to keep track of where you are up to and how you got there.

As you move across the page tracking your position with theirs, it allows you to summarize accurately and ensure that your facts are clear when you come to write up the agreement. Over time the record of offers allows you to:

| Issue | Yours | Theirs | Yours | Theirs | Yours | Theirs |
|---|---|---|---|---|---|---|
| Price/case | £14.90 | £12.20 | £14.50 | £13.00 | | £13.60 |
| Volume discount | 1.5% | 2.0% | 1.75% | 2.0% | | |
| Marketing investment | £80,000 | £150,000 | | £100,000 | | |
| Payment terms | 30 | 60 | 60 | | | |
| Distribution | 500 | 400 | | 500 | | |
| Volumes/pa | 1,000,000 | 1,000,000 | 1,300,000 | 1,500,000 | | |
| Promotions | 6 | 8 | 10 | 10 | | |
| Exclusivity | 12 months | 12 months | | | | |

**Figure 9.9** Record of offers.

- monitor the size of the moves they have made and on which variables;
- summarize across the variables with your running total of your last position;

If you don't confirm what you have agreed to, how do you know what decisions were actually made? In many cases, this can lead to yet another negotiation later on.

Now you are ready to negotiate. The planning is done, the tactics understood, the behaviors tuned and the thinking from inside their head in motion allowing you to see the deal opportunities as the other party sees them.

The Complete Skilled Negotiator is only as complete as is their planning, and never so complete that they can take anything for granted. Never assuming and always enquiring. Never rushed, always considered and respectful. It's a tough balance requiring nerve, confidence and tenacity and it is for this reason you can never afford to be complacent.

## CONCLUSION

Your ability to build agreements, dissolve deadlock situations, pre-condition expectations and close sustainable deals requires all of the skills, attributes, knowledge and self-awareness we have covered in *The Negotiation Book.*

For many, the challenges presented by negotiation do not come naturally and, as with any performance coupled with your own motivation to continuously improve, you have one of the most rewarding (in so many ways) personal development opportunities available to you.

Negotiating effectively is firstly about you accepting that it is only you who can influence the situations you are faced with. You can blame the market, personalities, timing, your options, the power balance or any circumstance that you may think happens to be working against you, but ultimately it is you who can turn around situations and make what would otherwise be deadlock situations into workable and profitable deals.

It is time to stay calm, see the tactics for what they are and exercise nerve and patience. Power real or perceived, however generated, will play its part in your negotiations and, no matter how good you are as a negotiator, where the balance of power is against you or your circumstances, you will no doubt experience the frustration of feeling of being compromised. Trust your instinct, exercise composure. It will make the difference between those agreements where you create value and those where you simply distribute it.

If you have to take a time-out, adjourn the meeting or go back and revisit the options, the fact that you recognize this and are prepared to take the time necessary is an indication that you are now behaving in an appropriate and conscious manner.

Know what you are trying to achieve and always try to work out what they are trying to achieve. This requires clarity in purpose and an acceptance, for those who are competitive in nature, that negotiation is not about winning, it is about letting them have your way, and to do this you must see the deal as they do.

Taking control of any situation requires planning and never is this as true as in negotiation. Negotiators who find themselves reacting to their environment and situation tend to place themselves in weaker positions than necessary. Always try to be as proactive and prepared as possible. It is the one thing you can do to enhance your prospects.

Self-awareness is probably the one dimension that differentiates the performance of the Complete Skilled Negotiator from others. They are not driven by fairness or consumed by their own ego. They and you should do that which is appropriate having weighed and considered each set of circumstances you are faced with.

To listen, think and reflect and to understand those around you and then consciously apply those skills we have learnt is what hopefully I have been able to promote and explain in this account of *The Negotiation Book*.

Negotiation is like no other skill. I know from my experience as well as that of my team, my clients and my family, that it can offer huge and well-earned rewards for anyone ready to become the Complete Skilled Negotiator.

# Index